The Red Mirror

THE RED MIRROR

Children of China's
Cultural Revolution

CHIHUA WEN

edited by Bruce Jones

with a foreword by Richard P. Madsen

Westview Press
Boulder • San Francisco • Oxford

Copyright © 1995 by Chihua Wen and Bruce Jones

Published in 1995 in the United States of America by Westview Press, Inc., 5500 Central Avenue, Boulder, Colorado 80301-2877, and in the United Kingdom by Westview Press, 36 Lonsdale Road, Summertown, Oxford OX2 7EW

Library of Congress Cataloging-in-Publication Data
Wen, Chihua.
    The red mirror : children of China's Cultural Revolution / Chihua Wen ; edited by Bruce Jones with a foreword by Richard P. Madsen.
      p.   cm.
    ISBN 0-8133-2489-0 — ISBN 0-8133-2488-2 (pbk.)
    1. China—History—Cultural Revolution, 1966–1969—Personal narratives.   I. Jones, Bruce.   II. Title.
DS778.7.W45   1995
951.05'6—DC20   94-29828
                                                                              CIP

Printed and bound in the United States of America

      The paper used in this publication meets the requirements
(∞) of the American National Standard for Permanence of Paper
      for Printed Library Materials Z39.48-1984.

10   9   8   7   6   5   4   3   2   1

Dedicated to my mother and my father,
who tried very hard to keep the evils of my own society
far from my brother and me even while they were consigned
to purgatory by the Party they thought they were serving

Ancient mirrors are supposed to have magic power to protect their owners from evil. They are believed to make hidden spirits visible and reveal the secrets of futurity.

Ch'in Shih Huang, the first Emperor of the Chin dynasty, a.d. 255, was credited with the possession of a magic mirror, which had the power of reflecting the inward parts of those who looked upon it.

Li Shih-min, a.d. 597–649, the second Emperor of the T'ang dynasty, is recorded to have remarked, "By using a mirror of brass you may see to adjust your cap; by using antiquity as a mirror, you may learn to foresee the rise and fall of Empires."

—**Encyclopedia of Chinese Symbolism and Art Motives**

Contents

THE STORIES

Foreword

RICHARD P. MADSEN

More important for the destiny of a society than the machinations of its politicians, the power of its armies, or the size of its police forces is the climate of opinion that sustains its common hopes. For instance, as Franz Schurmann put it, "the Soviet colossus was brought down not by foreign defeat, revolution in the streets, or fatal factional disputes but by a profound loss of spiritual faith. Ironically for a system that prided itself on atheism and materialism, it turned out to be critically dependent on this faith. Communism was a kind of religion, and when people stopped believing in it, they withdrew their support and the colossus fell." But how does a whole society lose its faith? Surely changes in a collective consciousness are the aggregation of millions of small breaking points, moments in time when individual men and women realize that they can no longer believe, that their old notions of what was good and effective no longer make sense.

Often, we can trace these small breaking points to some great collectively experienced trauma. China's Cultural Revolution was certainly such a collective trauma, leading eventually to a national loss of faith in communist ideology. After the Cultural Revolution, even though the Chinese Communist Party (CCP) continued to govern China, it could no longer plausibly claim to represent a historical vanguard; to stay in power, it had to adopt economic policies that contradicted its basic principles. But how do great collective traumas like the Cultural Revolution actually cause the individual breaking points in belief that together lead to a fundamental shift in national consciousness?

This collection of poignant stories is about a handful of such breaking points, episodes when Chinese individuals at a formative time in their lives severed the crucial strand of connection with the fabric of beliefs that connected them to the Chinese communist ideological system. Although each breaking point is different, they have important common features.

In each case, the crucial link is not a thick rope of ideas connecting the mind to the state but a delicate filament connecting the heart to a member of the family. Each of the individuals who tell their stories here was only a child or adolescent at the time of the Cultural Revolution. They remember believing at first that they would be properly connected to their Chinese "motherland" by being properly connected to their mothers and fathers. In each case, this belief was put to the test. Parents were condemned as "rightists," "capitalist roaders," or "counterrevolutionaries." Children had to decide whether to side with forces representing the motherland or with their real mothers and fathers. Sometimes the children participated in denunciation; other times they did what they could to shield their parents. If they did participate in harming their parents, they carried a burden of guilt that debilitated their connections to the larger social system. If they helped their parents, they harbored a bitter core of cherished defiance that they called on sometimes to resist too close a commitment to their would-be leaders.

In each case, the decisive event, the thing that became the focal point of their stories twenty years later, was not necessarily something of extraordinary material or practical importance, but something of great symbolic significance. A girl killed her pet hen to make chicken soup for her imprisoned father. Another girl made her grandmother destroy a cherished family heirloom. A boy melted down the incense burner his mother used to worship the Buddha. These violations of the idiosyncratic symbolic economy of a family's loyalties, mutual responsibility, and affection became the defining moments after which the moral bonds most intimately connected with a person's identity were never the same again.

"The Cultural Revolution," said the Maoists, "is a great revolution that touches men's very souls." In these stories, the events that most profoundly touched souls and in the end had the greatest influence on history were not the public "great" events—the purges of top Party officials, the mobilization of the Red Guards, battles between Red Guard factions, the downfall of Lin Biao—but domestic "great" events played out in the homely details of household life. However, to fully appreciate the lessons that these stories hold about the importance of this reduction of great events to domestic scale, we need to read the stories with some awareness of the great events occurring in the background.

The Cultural Revolution began in late 1965 with Mao Zedong's attempts to topple high-level Party members who were surreptitiously criticizing him through publication of literary works (including the series of stories about the Three Family Village in the *Beijing Evening News* mentioned in the Author's Introduction). In the early part of 1966, however, crucially placed officials managed to contain the criticism to a few allegedly disloyal writers and artists without implicating the high Party officials who supported the ideas expressed in the literary works. Mao took this as an indication that important leaders in the Party were arrayed against him. He and his associates came to believe that the Party was thoroughly infiltrated with people who, even though they might have been lifelong communists, had given up the ideals of true communism and "followed the capitalist road."

Supposedly the Party was so full of disloyal communists that it could not be trusted to carry out its own purge. So Mao and his associates attempted to launch mass movements of young people to attack wayward Party members. The organization of "Red Guard" groups of university students began in June 1966. Led by Party "work teams," under the direction of China's number two leader, Liu Shaoqi, these Red Guards attacked university administrators and teachers but—the Maoists later claimed—did not pursue the high-level Party officials who were primarily responsible for the disloyalty. By August 1966, Mao had taken charge, called on China's youth to "bombard the headquarters" of the Party, and convened a Party congress packed with his supporters to launch a mass movement that would indeed "touch people's very souls." The earliest stories in this collection begin after this date.

The fall of 1966 saw the creation of grassroots Red Guard (composed of students) and revolutionary Rebel (composed of workers) groups throughout the country. Partly because of the machinations of top officials still desperately seeking to hold on to their power, these Red Guards and revolutionary Rebels directed the first phase of their attacks against intellectuals supposedly affected with foreign ideas and against the "Four Olds"—old customs, habits, thinking, and culture. It was during this time that Chihua Wen's neighbor had all his books burned; the poet father of the narrator of "Poems and Pigs" was denounced for writing books full of "poisonous weeds"; and the narrator of "Iron Grandma" forced the grandmother to burn the precious old imperial exam written by the narrator's grandfather toward the end of the Qing dynasty.

By the end of the fall of 1966, the Red Guard and Rebel groups had split into "conservative" (or Black) and "radical" (or Red) factions. The conservatives were mainly the children of Party officials, and they aimed to carry out their revolution in a way that would spare privileged political figures such as their parents. The radicals were youths who came from "bad" family backgrounds—their parents had been landlords, intellectuals, businesspeople, or officials of the Kuomintang (KMT) government before the 1949 Revolution, or they had been branded as rightists during the 1957 campaign against people who had made unacceptable criticisms of the Communist Party. Like the narrator of "Class Origins," children from such bad-class backgrounds were stigmatized and faced a bleak future in the People's Republic of China. But the early rhetoric of the Cultural Revolution gave hope to such young people. If they could zealously carry out the aims of the Cultural Revolution, denounce their "capitalist" family members, and tear down the bastions of privilege within the Party, they might be able to redeem their bad backgrounds and become true revolutionary heroes. Like the narrator of "Class Origins," many such youths tried to do this. But in the end, the leaders of the Cultural Revolution reaffirmed the importance of bloodlines. A person who had not been born Red could never be truly Red. Thus, those radical Red youths who betrayed their parents did not benefit politically from their actions.

Since the Red Guards and the Rebels were grassroots organizations, they could not be tightly controlled by leaders in Beijing. Mao and his associates could guide the direction of the Cultural Revolution only loosely. They attempted this guidance by alternately giving a green light to the radical and conservative Red Guards and Rebels. Around January 1967, the radicals were encouraged to carry out "power seizures" of top government organizations. Officials were deposed from office, publicly humiliated, sometimes tortured. Such was the fate of the fathers of the narrators of "Prisoners and Wardens," "Butterflies and Rain," "Sustaining Life," and "No Adolescence." Then, alarmed by the threat of anarchy posed by these power seizures, in the late winter and early spring of 1967 the Cultural Revolution's leaders in Beijing threw their support to the more conservative Red Guard and Rebel factions. By the summer of 1967, however, the leaders had swung the tide back toward radicalism. But by then upper-level supporters of both radicals and conservatives had allowed them access to weapons from military armories. The summer of 1967 was a time of bloody anarchic violence as different Red Guard and Rebel factions carried out "armed struggle" against one another. Most of the remaining stories in this collection took place at this time. The armed violence was especially fierce in Chengdu, where about half of the narrators, including the one in "Familiar Weapons," come from. By this time, much of the violence seemed to take on a logic of its own, a rhythm of vendetta and countervendetta little connected with any of the ideological goals originally proclaimed for the Cultural Revolution. Many of the stories based on events during this time period seem to be describing arbitrarily inflicted disasters, all the more horrifying because of their meaninglessness.

By the autumn of 1967, the People's Liberation Army (PLA) had moved in to suppress the uncontrolled violence and establish order throughout the country. Various pockets of violence persisted into 1968, however. And somewhat more organized but no less grisly purges continued through 1968. Victims of these purges were often imprisoned without any kind of due process in locally constructed jails called "cowsheds." Other people toppled from authority were sent to labor reform camps. A May 7, 1968, directive established the May 7 Cadre Schools—rural reform camps where former government officials were sent for indefinite stays to learn peasant virtues by doing manual labor and proper ideology by studying and discussing Cultural Revolution documents. In this process, fathers and mothers were separated from each other and from their children. Later, separations were increased when urban youths were forcibly sent to live in villages in the countryside. A number of the stories are about young people struggling to get back in touch with their parents after such separations.

Behind all of the frenetic top-level political maneuvering and the chaotic grassroots violence were struggles over basic issues. Two of the most important were privilege and community. As the Maoists saw the matter, a fundamental goal of their revolution had been equality. They professed outrage at the persistence of privilege in the People's Republic: the remnants of privilege still enjoyed by the old bourgeoisie and (hypocritically in view of the lavish lifestyle of top Cultural Revolution leaders such as Jiang Qing, Mao's wife) the new privileges claimed by high-ranking Party members. The Maoists also decried the cooling of China's revolutionary fervor, the preference of Chinese citizens for a harmonious and comfortable life among family and friends rather than for continued revolutionary struggle and self-sacrifice. The Maoists wanted to create an aroused national community of "revolutionary successors" who eschewed family feeling and friendship for comradeship under the cultlike leadership of Mao Zedong.

The narrators of these stories suffered because they represented privilege. Their houses were spacious. They had servants. Their families rubbed shoulders with the locally famous and powerful. Their privileges were mostly those of China's Party elites. Some of the narrators' families had come from prerevolutionary upper classes—merchants, scholars, officers in the KMT army. The family of "Iron Grandma" had even been part of the Qing dynasty's imperial officialdom. But most of these people had joined the revolution well before the communist victory in 1949. They were now members of the communist establishment. At the time the events in the stories happened, the narrators were very young, between about six and thirteen. Perhaps because of their youth, most of the narrators did not join Red Guard organizations. But if they had, they would have belonged to the conservative factions that worked to protect former power holders. (Exceptions are the families in "Class Origins," "Familiar Weapons," and "For a Little Love.") Most of the families of the narrators were pulled down by radical Red Guards jealous of the benefits claimed by the communist establishment in a land still plagued by scarcity.

As the radical Red Guards struggled against such families, they tried to get the children to denounce their parents and thus demonstrate that their true commitment was not to family but to the Revolution led by Mao. Perhaps because many of the narrators were so young, too young to be "enlisted" in the struggle against family, they were simply dragged along, bewildered and frightened, into the misery of their families' fates. Some of the young people in these stories did, however, turn against their parents. Partly out of adolescent rebellion, partly out of opportunism, the narrator of "Familiar Weapons," who was thirteen at the time, joined a radical Red Guard faction (the Hong Cheng), acquired some weapons, and actually confronted his father with a gun. The narrator of "Class Origins" informed local leaders that his bad-class father had "problems coping with the revolution"; as a result his father was beaten until half paralyzed.

It is one of the bitter ironies of the Cultural Revolution that for all of its rhetoric against traditional family and kinship ties, it ultimately reinforced them. For in the end, its leaders affirmed a "blood theory" of Redness: No one could be truly Red who came from a bad-class background. No matter what one's political performance, one could not escape the fate of one's family. Moreover, if one family member was labeled an enemy of the Revolution, all the rest of the family had to suffer

as well. Those who tried to "draw a clear line" between themselves and
their parents gained nothing from their betrayal. It was as if they had
sold their souls to the devil and were not even paid for them.

Thus, in spite of past conflicts and traumas, the narrators of these
stories all retain a deep connection to their parents. Because of those
conflicts and traumas, it is a connection colored variously by sorrow,
anger, guilt, and remorse. This familial attachment is juxtaposed with
an ironic detachment from the public realm, which had imposed impossible demands and inflicted senseless suffering. The family relationship seems the only really important relationship in the narrators' lives,
the only thing that makes sense where politics and public life have been
discredited.

What the Chinese called the "Cultural Revolution era" came to a
close in 1976 with the death of Mao and the overthrow of those who
were his closest accomplices in the upheaval. The new leaders of China
were those members of the Party establishment whom the Cultural
Revolution had sought to overthrow. Most of the parents portrayed in
these stories who were not killed in the upheaval probably received their
positions back. Most of their children now seem to be doing quite well
in China: They are journalists, writers, teachers, officials, entrepre-
neurs.

What seem to characterize their generation are a wariness toward
public affairs, a distrust of government promises, a buried hostility. "I
will never forgive them," the closing line of "Prisoners and Wardens," is
perhaps the sentiment that summarizes this generation's attitude toward
the persons responsible for all this suffering. But the person who silently feels that sentiment does not rebelliously confront the officials
implicated in her mother's torment. She simply stands motionless, staring at them with her hands clasped behind her back. Afterward, she and
her brothers presumably go about their lives, sustained and comforted
by the memory of their mother.

This collection of stories, then, mostly represents a generation whose
relatively privileged families had deep communist roots. Because of the
Cultural Revolution, those roots are now dead. But they still keep this

generation—whose members are now in their mid-thirties to early forties and are the natural leaders of contemporary China—grounded in place, averse to any more adventures of rebellious defiance. Perhaps this is why China is a society that has given up socialism without admitting it, that commingles political conservatism with economic dynamism, that is thoroughly pragmatic and places little stock in ideological consistency, that solves problems not through confrontation but through evasion, that conducts its affairs through networks of family and friends and places little faith in public institutions. This book shows us a few of the defining moments that, in giving this key generation its characteristic mentality, have set the moral tone for contemporary China.

Acknowledgments

If these stories touch people or inspire them to learn more about China, it is because my brothers and sisters in China made the heartbreaking events of their lives available to me. To my childhood friends who shared their lives and stories with me, I owe a debt that I hope telling their stories repays in some measure.

Not all of these stories came from my friends. Some stories came from people referred by my friends. So I owe another debt to my friends, especially Xiaoying Hua, my friend in the United States. Xiaoying sent letters to her friends in Beijing; because of her, I was able to talk to many more people than I would have by relying only on my own resources.

If readers of the book find the stories easy reading, it is because of Bruce Jones, my first reader and editor, who helped me conceive of the idea for this book and bring all the stories to their best advantage. For his support, love, patience, and frank criticism, I am grateful.

I am also indebted to Dick Madsen for his suggestions and advice. His friendship and his knowledge of Chinese culture helped lead this project in the right direction.

Finally I want to say, "Thank you" to two people at Westview Press: to Susan McEachern, for her sharp eyes, which saw the value in this work, and to Jane Raese, for her hard work and cooperation, which brought this project to a conclusion.

Chihua Wen

AUTHOR'S
INTRODUCTION

IN PRIMARY SCHOOL, our teachers taught us that our Chinese motherland was a huge garden and that children like ourselves were flowers in that garden. I took that metaphor to heart and thought that I, along with all my brothers and sisters, would become something bright—flowers or trees—in the garden, testaments to the glory of China. We never planned on the horrible storm that would howl through every corner of the country and sweep the garden bare. That storm was the Great Proletarian Cultural Revolution.

The Cultural Revolution started the summer I turned eight years old. As a child, I saw young people die in the streets. When I first saw someone die from gunfire in the streets, I was terrified. When I saw a second, third, or fourth death, I got used to it. Talking with my friends about the street fighting and death became like talking about food. While bread is a necessary part of life, violent death in the streets should not be. During the Cultural Revolution, death was a part of nearly every child's life.

In 1966, I was in a second-grade class in the most prestigious elementary school in Chengdu, the capital city of China's Sichuan Province. Children in China are taught to obey authority from the first day they walk into school. As in all classrooms in China, above the chalkboard in our room was a portrait of Mao Zedong. My second-grade teacher used to tell us, "Chairman Mao is watching every day to see who is a Red child and who is not." Whenever a child acted naughtily in the classroom, the teacher would ask rhetorically, "Who is watching?" We knew she meant Chairman Mao.

Schools and other social institutions constantly reminded children that the new China could not exist without the Party. Authority was concretized by the creation of revolutionary martyrs and heroes. Teachers reminded us that we would not be sitting in such bright and peaceful classrooms if the revolutionary martyrs had not shed their blood for us. The first hint of the Revolution came at school. One morning my Chinese teacher, normally a happy, pretty young woman, walked into the classroom with a serious look on her face. Instead of picking one or two of us to recite the text assigned the day before, she said something I did not understand about Deng Tuo, Wu Han, and Liao Mosha. She called them San Jia Cun, the Three Family Village, and criticized them for being counterrevolutionaries who worked against the Party.

The teacher then divided the class into groups to rehearse a small play she had written denouncing Deng, Wu, and Liao. My role in the play was to recite these lines:

> *Deng Tuo, Wu Han, Liao Mosha,*
> *Three from the same family.*
> *Anti-Party, Anti–Chairman Mao.*
> *The Three Family Village*
> *Is a revisionist Black family.*

While speaking these lines, I was to stamp my right foot on the platform and point my finger at three of my classmates who were playing Deng, Wu, and Liao.

ℰℛ

Before we could even write politically charged characters such as "revisionist" correctly, or understand their meanings, our teachers had us using these harsh political terms. We may not have known what the terms meant, but we knew they were bad words. Every time my teacher said, "Revisionist," she had a distasteful look on her face. When she coached me for my part in the play, she constantly reminded me to speak loudly and to act indignantly.

While we were using these words in our small dramas in school, and later in the streets when we wished to taunt each other, it never occurred to us that the intellectuals, writers, and artists we were denouncing were people like our own parents—people like Deng, Wu, Liao, and others who would later be singled out and denounced as revisionists. Lacking the ability to distinguish between good people and bad people, we were unaware we were creating "Enemies of the Party" among ourselves.

One day I came home from the rehearsal of a new play at school and asked my father what revisionist and bourgeois meant. He answered that they were words that should not be used carelessly. I did not know then that my father had already been attacked as a bourgeois writer. Nor did I know this was why I had been assigned to play a villain in the current play.

Like many of my friends' and schoolmates' parents, my parents were accused by the Party of being counterrevolutionaries. And like many members of my generation, I suddenly found myself not knowing whom to believe, my parents or the Party. We struggled to cope with the conflict of loving our parents and at the same time trying to follow the Party's call to be Red successors to the Revolution.

Our parents had ill-equipped us for this task. They had taught us to obey the Party and its representatives—our teachers and the other school authorities. It was the job of our teachers to teach us what was good and what was bad.

Like myself, almost every child I knew was a member of Shaoxiandui, the Young Pioneers, by the time she or he was ten years old. Young Pioneers wore a triangular red scarf, which signified both a corner of the national flag and the blood of the revolutionary martyrs. We all raised our right hands under the Red flag, making a solemn vow to follow the Chinese Communist Party and to be a Communist Successor. Along the way we sang the theme song of the Young Pioneers:

> *Are you ready?*
> *We are always ready.*
> *We are the Communist Children's Corps.*
> *We will be masters of the future.*

From childhood on, we were indoctrinated into what it meant to be chosen as a Red successor. Red successors were protected by the Party, loyal to their parents, and loyal to the Party. The teachers told us that communism was our life goal and our future. To be a Red successor to Mao, "you must be a member of the Communist Party after you grow up," the teacher often told us. Joining the Young Pioneers was the first step. Next was joining the Communist Youth League. Many parents tried to force their children to be members. They were afraid of what might happen if their children did not participate in the rituals of a good communist childhood.

ℰↃ

One evening in the autumn of 1966, I joined a group of kids talking in the compound where I lived. A teenage boy was saying that his sister had seen a poster on a wall in the commercial center of the city. The boy was acting strangely, as if he should keep quiet. We asked him what the slogan said. He did not want to talk, but we pushed him and insisted that he tell us. He lowered his voice and said, "Down with Liu Shaoqi, the Khrushchev of China."

Everyone got very silent. No one responded. We looked around the circle at each other. Finally another boy asked him, "Are you sure the name was Liu Shaoqi? Maybe you didn't hear your sister properly."

Now that he had spoken, the teenager was confident of his information. "I'm positive," he said.

We exchanged glances again. All of a sudden, we began to discuss whether the slogan was counterrevolutionary. I said that photographs of Liu Shaoqi in the newspapers always showed him standing next to Chairman Mao. Another girl, much older than me, said that was why he was the Khrushchev of China. Liu Shaoqi was the Party chairman and head of the country at the time.

Someone suggested that we go to see, so we ran down to see the poster. It was still on the wall, and a crowd had gathered. Everyone seemed to be talking about whether Liu was a time bomb beside Chairman Mao. I did not really understand the metaphor, but I remembered the movie *Ten O'Clock on National Day*, which showed a KMT spy who attempted to assassinate Mao by placing a time bomb in a public place where Mao would be.

When I got home from the wall, I told my parents what I had seen. My father's first reaction was stunned silence. My mother said, "You are too young to understand what you saw. You should stay at home from now on." Then my father said, "You should stay a child. You have the rest of your life to be an adult and to worry about the things you don't understand today."

Despite my father's cautions, life in the outside world was far too interesting for me to let it slide by. My friends and I had many reasons and opportunities to think about what was happening in China.

During the late summer and through the fall of 1966, the newspapers were full of stories about the almost 2 million young people traveling to Beijing to gather with other Red Guards in Tiananmen Square and waiting for Mao to appear over the Gate of Heavenly Peace and render his benediction. The streets of Chengdu were full of young people saying that to see Mao and to be seen by him were recognition that one was a true son or daughter of communism, a Red successor to the Revolution.

One of my neighbors, Li-li was the daughter of a well-known historian. Li-li was part of the first group of Red Guards to travel to Beijing to be received by Mao. When she came home from Beijing, Li-li told her friends she was no longer afraid of anybody. Mao had bestowed his blessing on her, and no one could accuse her of being Black simply because her father had been persecuted during the Antirightist Campaign.

She encouraged the rest of us to go to Beijing and march for Mao. Five of us decided to go. I ran home and stuck a few clothes in my schoolbag and then dashed to the railway station to meet my comrades. We did not have to worry about money because the Red Guards had already commandeered the trains in the name of the Revolution. The Red Guards were happy to transport all of China's youths to Beijing to show their support for Mao.

The railway platform was the first indication that China was at war. It seemed as though everyone in town was trying to squeeze onto the train. One of my older friends said it looked like a scene from *War and Peace*. This started an argument about which author was best at describing revolution. I liked Hugo and another friend was partial to Gorky. Unable to get close to the train, we stood arguing, as though we were at the train station to debate literature instead of going to Beijing to see Mao. We argued until our parents arrived and took us home. I never did figure out how my father found out about our plans.

Even though we never got to Beijing to see Mao, we were excited by the Party's call to revolution and the newspaper photos of Mao reviewing the Red Guards in Tiananmen. We had no real experience with revolution. We thought it was our turn, our moment, our chance to move away from the established order and contribute to a new China, our chance to march, fists in the air, shouting political slogans and making our loyalty to the Party visible. We were good; they—anyone who dared disagree with us—were evil. We would be Red Guards; we would guard Mao's thoughts, guard the Party's principles, and, above all, guard the communist ideology. We felt grown up overnight. With Mao's blessing, we became the masters of society; we controlled life; we determined our fate rather than the other way around.

Even though my friends and I were not yet Red Guards, we envisioned ourselves as the revolutionaries we had already seen in movies. While the five of us who had planned to run away to Beijing enjoyed our delusion of becoming Red Guards, their leadership was already making plans that would exclude us because of our parents' backgrounds.

In the early stages of the Cultural Revolution, anyone who wanted to could join the Red Guards as long as he or she was middle-school age (early teens) or older. Later, two categories were established to determine who could join the Red Guards. There were five Red categories: workers, poor and lower-middle peasants, revolutionary soldiers, revolutionary martyrs, and revolutionary cadres who had joined the Party before 1949. Opposite to the five Red categories were five Black categories for those to be excluded: former landlords, rich peasants, counterrevolutionaries (including former members of the KMT), bad elements, and rightists. The five Black categories were actually seven if one included the bourgeoisie and capitalist roaders (people in power who preferred the capitalist way of life). Youths born to Black families were not admitted to the Red Guards unless they proved that they had renounced their class and denounced their parents.

The importance of blood is different in China than in the West. In the West, family members enjoy an independence that is not found in China. For instance, when a parent in the West commits a crime, the children do not automatically become criminals as a result. At a theoretical level, the same holds true in China, but the opposite is true in reality. Once a parent is accused of a political crime, all her or his children are equally suspect.

> *A dragon conceives a dragon,*
> *And a phoenix conceives a phoenix.*
> *A rat gives birth to a rat*
> *While digging in the dirt.*

It was a short step from accusing parents to publicly humiliating children for the mistake of being born into a Black family. It did not even help if the parents had disowned their own family and joined the Party before the Revolution. Working-class children and those of the peasants became automatically superior to those from intellectual and former landholding families.

Older youths from the now-labeled Black families who had joined the Red Guards at the beginning, who had traveled to Beijing, and who had been received by Mao were now being kicked out of the brigades. This was more than being asked to leave a club. Just as the the red kerchief of the Young Pioneers was a necessary badge of a Red successor, the armband of the Red Guard was the mark of a good person. To be turned out of the guard was to be condemned as a criminal.

These new notions of class fit neatly with Mao's earlier rhetoric. In his attempts to control intellectual elements in the Party, Mao had repeatedly drawn distinctions between good art and bad art. Good art was created by the workers, peasants, and soldiers and served their needs. Bad art was created to celebrate intellectual activity and ignored the masses. These distinctions were used to attack the Three Family Village writers who were ventriloquizing the politics of more powerful leaders of the Beijing Central Committee.

These same distinctions would now be turned against intellectuals and artists at every level of Chinese society by the Red Guard units. These notions provided grounds for accusation, denunciation, and persecution of anyone who was not a worker, peasant, or soldier. All the petty jealousies of the masses could now be directed, funneled into hatred, and used to destroy China's educated minority. Such class discrimination gave rise to atrocities perpetrated against the Black families. These atrocities in turn fanned the flames of more class hatred.

The children of Red families were entitled to rebel and destroy whatever and whomever they did not like in the name of the Revolution. They were encouraged to attack the Four Olds: old ideas, old culture, old habits, and old customs. These attacks occurred everywhere.

The concept of the Four Olds was broad. The lack of focus and definition made things confusing. Anything from before the 1949 Revolution could be taken as old. Anyone found in possession of goods from that period could, and frequently did, suffer horrible consequences. The Red Guards raided private houses without warning, turning the household inside out, throwing "bourgeois" possessions such as jewelry, Western-style clothing, women's high heels, and *qipao* into the street, making everyone's shame public.[1]

Frequently these items were dug from the closets and chests of intellectuals who otherwise wore the politically fashionable clothing of Mao jackets and the baggy blue pants of the workers. The intellectuals hid

---

1. A *qipao* is a traditional Chinese woman's dress, which dates to the Qing dynasty and its Manchurian influence on fashion. Usually made of brocaded silk, a *qipao* has a high neck, a close-fitting bodice, and long slit up both sides of the skirt. The *qipao* was labeled part of the Four Olds during the Cultural Revolution. It was seen as a symbol of feudalism.

their old clothing at home and would take it out occasionally to look at or dress in as a means of escaping the political pressures of the day and being themselves for a while. This proved to be a dangerous practice because when the Red Guards discovered the outlawed items, their owners were accused of being unwilling to discard their traditional morals and of disapproving of the Party's attitude that clothing should reflect the demands of laboring people's lives. At first, people took to removing the shoulder pads from Western suit coats and women's dresses to make them less conspicuous. Others cut off the high heels on their shoes. Eventually, the Red Guards' search raids were so threatening that many families simply threw their "old" Western-style clothing in the trash.

Destroying one's Olds by oneself did not necessarily guarantee safety. A friend of my family's, a woman from a wealthy Christian family, had burned her collection of traditional Chinese paintings and calligraphy and thrown away her Western clothes. The only things she had kept were a jade charm given her by her grandmother and her mother's Bible. Her grandmother had promised that the charm would protect her from the devil, and her mother had told her that the Bible would keep evil away.

Then, before the Red Guards could come to raid her house, she went to a department store to get some material to make herself a suitable, proletarian-looking outfit. There were only two kinds of cloth in the store. Both were a stiff denim, one plain and the other with a flower pattern. She purchased several yards of the flower-patterned denim and used it to make a skirt and blouse. The next day, calm and prepared, she put on her new proletarian clothing and waited for the raid.

The sky was getting dark when seven Red Guards broke into her house. They emptied all the closets and dresser drawers, looking for something old. Angry when they did not find anything, one grabbed her by her collar and threw her to the floor. The Red Guards then stood around her in a circle, accusing her of destroying the evidence of her guilt. One of the guards, a girl of about fifteen, screamed, "How dare you disguise yourself as one of the proletariat? Do you think we cannot tell who you are just because you wear denim? We are Chairman Mao's Red Guards, and we have very discerning eyes. Flowered denim? You are deliberately bringing shame on the proletarian class."

The woman asked the girl, "Is it wrong to be neat?" The Red Guards responded by hacking off her hair in the *ying yang tou* style, where the hair on one half of the head was chopped short and the hair on the other half was shaved clean.

Before the Cultural Revolution, I thought that being abducted or arrested was something that happened only to criminals and to characters in the movies. It never occurred to me that I would be witness to such things.

Those ideas changed the evening I watched my next-door neighbors get abducted by the Red Guards. They were well-known revolutionary writers and had been in Yan'an in the 1930s as members of the Party. Before the Cultural Revolution, Yan'an was regarded as the cradle of the Chinese Communist Party, and anyone who had been there was seen as as a quintessential revolutionary. Now this counted for nothing.

It was dusk when a truck stopped in front of our apartment building. A group of teenagers wearing Red Guard armbands kicked their way into the apartment. My friends and I were playing outside, and we stopped to watch. At that time we were still too young and innocent to be frightened enough to run away.

The sound of breaking glass and a child's screaming burst from the apartment. In a few minutes three Red Guards emerged from the apartment with a gunnysack. They dumped the contents into the courtyard—books. They set the books on fire. I noticed that one was a collection of Robert Browning's poetry.

Two of the Red Guards went back into the building, while the third stood guard over the fire. The books were almost burnt to ashes when the Red Guards came back out of the apartment carrying two more gunnysacks. The sacks were so heavy it took three of the young men to carry each one. As they threw the sacks into the truck, I heard the sound of gagging. The guards jumped into the truck and sped away. No one ever saw my next-door neighbors again.

Shortly after I witnessed this abduction, the news came that the working classes had begun forming their own groups, called the Red Rebels. The first such group to appear was the Association of Red Rebels, which arose in Beijing in the winter of 1967.

Following the advent of the Association of Red Rebels, many similar organizations sprang up throughout the country, with names such as East Is Red, Rebel to the End, or the Mao Zedong Thought Red Guards. Just as new groups that claimed to follow Mao were forming to oppose the Red Guards, these Rebels were being resisted by other militant organizations of workers that claimed they represented Mao's line. Almost all the factories in the country went on strike. The railway workers, after obligingly carrying millions of Red Guards to Beijing for free, now took control of all trains in the country, declaring that they would now travel free to Beijing to establish their revolutionary ties with one another. While seeing Mao was the reason the Red Guards went to Beijing, by the time the Rebels began to travel, Mao had long discontinued the practice of appearing in front of the crowds at Tiananmen. The Rebels merely used this as an excuse for personal travel at the expense of the rest of the country.

The railway workers did not limit the free travel to their own union. In their rhetoric, they extended the privilege to any other workers' group as long as it was also a Rebel group supporting the thought of Mao Zedong. Ideologically, workers all belonged to the same class. In reality, anyone who enjoyed political power or who had connections with the railway workers got free travel. Everyone else stayed home.

Unlike the children of the Red Guard units, the Rebels were primarily from the rural areas and were poorly educated, fully grown adults. These Rebels frequently brought their entire families along when traveling for the Revolution. When they stopped for the night, they freely took over the residences of Black families and used them as they pleased.

I remember one spring night in 1967. The whole compound where I lived was suddenly filled with shouts. "Open up. Let us in, you horde of reactionaries," cried a group of Rebels at our gate. They would have climbed over the walls and into the courtyard if our old doorman had not appeared to let them in. Right away someone was pounding on our door. My grandmother opened it, and a handsome young man with his wife and sister walked into our house. He said that he was a newlywed and that the three of them were going to Beijing for their revolutionary honeymoon. Then he looked straight at my father and called him by name. He demanded that my father cook dinner for them. He wanted to know if a reactionary writer could cook like working-class people. My father was about to go into the kitchen when the young man changed his mind and ordered my mother to cook instead. Then he demanded that my father recite some of his poetry.

My father said, "I dare not. My poems have been criticized as poisonous weeds."

The young man laughed coldly and said, "This is a revolutionary Rebel ordering you. How dare you refuse? We know all your reactionary behavior very well. We want to criticize your poisonous writing now." Then he knocked my father to the floor and began kicking him in the stomach. Fortunately, he was stopped by his wife after the third kick. We could tell from his accent that he was from Chongqing.

The next day the courtyard of the compound was filled with dozens of young people with the same heavy Chongqing accent. One of our neighbors was a playwright. His house was occupied by seven Rebels: four men and three women. In the 1930s, this playwright had been in the underground Communist Party in Chongqing. After everyone left, he told us that, with his insight as a veteran Party member, he knew that someone in our compound was a Judas who had sold us out to the Rebels from Chongqing.

We found our Judas soon. He was a young working-class songwriter who was a failure at his trade. He had joined a Rebel organization in Chengdu for personal revenge. He thought of himself as a gifted songwriter whose failures could be traced to the bourgeois, reactionary intellectuals who had suppressed him. He joined the Rebels and wrote revolutionary songs. His rebellious comrades had connections with their counterparts in Chongqing, and he invited them to stay with us when they traveled through Chengdu.

A few weeks later this same Rebel forced my father to write my aunt in Shanghai to "welcome" and accommodate the Rebel. Our Judas was going to Shanghai with his comrades for the Revolution. Friends later told us that he forced them to do the same thing when he discovered they had relatives in other big cities where he and his friends wanted to travel.

Our revolutionary Rebel songwriter was no exception. At the stage when the working class mobilized itself as Rebels and was treated as the leading class again, members of other social groups began joining Rebel organizations, either seeking protection, showing their moral support for the new leading classes, or simply believing Mao when he said that it was right to rebel.

During the Cultural Revolution, class loyalty and identification meant nothing. As part of the Antirightist Campaign in 1957 a local writer had criticized the work of a famous poet. Early in the Revolution, he was attacked by the Red Guards. After the attack, he was told that the poet had a son who was a member of the Red Guards.

Later, when the working classes revolted and adult Rebel groups began to form, this writer joined a local Rebel organization. Soon a group of my friends and I saw the poet being carried home on a stretcher. His shirt was soaked in blood. His wife said his ribs had been broken in a beating by the Rebels.

გ

In the summer of 1967, my parents sent me to my aunt's house in the countryside to protect me from the violence in the city. My aunt's home sat on the crest of a hill, surrounded by orange trees. One morning as we were shucking corn in the yard, a young man in a white shirt covered with blood came up the hill. He begged my aunt to help him. She took the young man inside the house and shut the door behind her. A few minutes later she returned to her work.

Soon three men carrying pistols and wearing red armbands proclaiming, "The East Is Red" came up the hill. They asked my aunt if she had seen a young man passing by. She said, "Yes" and pointed down the hill toward town, away from the direction the men had come. The Rebels ran in the direction she pointed. My aunt took my hand, pulled me into the house, and closed the door.

"Where is that wounded man?" I asked. My aunt led me through the house, out the back door, across the yard, and into a storage lean-to. In the middle of the room were two coffins. My aunt and uncle had prepared coffins for themselves, a large one for him and a smaller one for her, in case anything happened to their children and someone else had to bury them.

I had never been this close to a coffin before. My aunt told me to help her open the smaller of the two. With shaking hands, we opened the coffin. There was the wounded young man. My aunt told him he should leave before the Rebels returned.

⌘

Once the Rebels seized power, they began the practice of *niu peng*, or the "cowshed"—places of confinement where they kept intellectuals and artists, completely isolating them from their families. The Rebels claimed that the intellectuals were being confined to the cowsheds to get their old brains reformed and cleaned up. This was to be accomplished by writing confessions and studying Mao's writings—the moral maxims of the whole society.

Calling the places of confinement cowsheds and locking up people were meant to dehumanize them. The rebels had a term for the people they locked in cowsheds: *niugui sheshen*. Literally the term meant "cow ghosts and snake spirits;" metaphorically it connoted monsters and demons—the forces of evil. During the Cultural Revolution, this term came to mean class enemies of all kinds.

This expression was not the Rebels' creation. It came from Mao, who loved to use metaphors and fables from Chinese literature. Mao took the phrase from a famous novel of the Qing dynasty, the *Travel Notes of*

Lao Can, written by Liu E, who used the phrase to refer to corrupt court and military officials.

During the Antirightist Campaign, Mao attacked the Shanghai newspaper *Wenhui Bao* for its bourgeois orientation. Mao said, "Only let cow ghosts and snake spirits come out of their places when it makes it easier to annihilate them; only let poisonous weeds break through the earth when it makes it more convenient to wipe them out."[2] The term *poisonous weeds* came to refer to any writing deemed dangerous to the Revolution. The Rebels appropriated the phrase *cow ghosts and snake spirits* in their attack on China's intellectuals. After imprisoning the intellectuals, the Rebels used the slogan "Sweep Away All Cow Ghosts and Snake Spirits" to dehumanize their charges.

One afternoon the Rebels opened a local cowshed and sent all the prisoners out to pick cotton in the fields while the prisoners' children watched them work. At noon the Rebels called a meeting at the field to criticize the intellectuals, who were lined up under the hot Sichuan sun. The Rebels began shouting their criticisms at their prisoners. My friends and I were attracted by the crowd drawn by the shouting. In the field the children of the prisoners followed the example of the Rebels and began berating their own fathers. One of them, a fourteen-year-old boy, carried a metal rod in his hand. He ordered the prisoners to stretch out their hands. One by one he slapped their palms with the rod while accusing them of being bourgeois because their hands were so smooth.

This boy's father received his beating in turn. When I asked the boy later how he could strike his own father, he replied that he was only beating "cow ghosts and snake spirits."

ల

In the fall of 1968 another poster appeared in Chengdu. This time it struck home. Hung on the wall of the compound where I lived, the new poster said:

---

2. Mao Tse-tung, *Talks at the Yenan Forum on Literature and Art,* 4th ed. (Peking: Foreign Languages Press, 1967).

THE LATEST DIRECTIVE OF CHAIRMAN MAO

Vast number of cadres should be transferred to do manual labor in the countryside. This is a chance for them to relearn the lessons of the masses. Apart from the aged, the weak, and the sick, all cadres should be sent to the countryside to facilitate their remolding. Cadres at their posts should be transferred in turn to the countryside to do manual labor.

I was too young to understand the meaning of Mao's directive but not too young to know that being sent to the countryside was punishment and not reform. Before the Antirightist Campaign, my uncle had been a manager for a large petroleum company. After he was accused of being a rightist in 1958, he was sent to the countryside along with his wife and children. They all became peasants overnight.

However, my friends and I were not frightened. We enjoyed day-dreaming about the future. Several of us were discussing the poster, verbally picturing the countryside, thinking our parents would look like the Russian revolutionaries in Tolstoy's *Resurrection* who were sent into exile in Siberia.

One boy said he had a Russian-style hat. He asked us to imagine how handsome he would be in some snowy forest, wearing the hat and his boots. I said I would definitely take my hooded red coat, a birthday gift from my father. Another boy, a little bit older than me, cut me off, saying "Oh, you little girl, you just want to be like Little Red Riding Hood. How do you know where our parents will be sent? How do you know the countryside will be any better than a cowshed?" His words caused silence. One thing we were certain of was that if the place our parents were sent was like a cowshed, we would not be allowed to follow.

The next day we learned that the place Mao wanted to send the cadres and intellectuals was called a Wu Qi Gan Xiao, a May 7 Cadre School, or Gan Xiao for short. The "May 7" part of the name was taken from May 7, 1968, when the Revolutionary Committee of Heilongjiang Province, in northeastern China, sent several dozen denounced intellectuals and capitalist roaders to a farm in Anqing County called Liuhe May Seventh Cadre School.

Several months later the *People's Daily* newspaper published an article about the experiment of reforming cadres through labor. The newspaper also published Mao's comments on the experiment in the same issue. Following the publication of Mao's remarks, the practice of sending intellectuals and other cadres to Gan Xiao spread across the country.

Each social institution and working unit had its own Gan Xiao. All were located in poor, remote rural areas. Soon the fears of that wise child in the courtyard came true. Our parents were sent to places in the countryside, and we were not allowed to follow. In cases like mine, where parents did not work for the same unit, mothers and fathers were sent to different camps.

Both my father and mother were in the first group of intellectuals to be sent from Chengdu. There was no consideration given for family or for health. Although my father suffered from severe asthma, he was sent to a Gan Xiao on the Vietnamese border. My mother was sent to a mountain area close to Tibet.

か

When my parents were sent to the countryside, they left me in a household that included my grandmother, who was in her sixties and not in good health, and my little brother. It fell to me to look after my brother. About a year and a half after my parents were sent away, my brother came down with hepatitis. After I bought the medicine and some sugar necessary to help my brother regain his health, there was too little money left to meet the rest of our needs. I told my grandmother that I had to go visit my mother. She asked me how I would get there without any money. I did not know.

Fortunately, I had a classmate named Li Yi whose parents had been sent to the same Gan Xiao as my mother. Her older brother had a friend who worked for the post office. She thought that he and his friends might be able to find a parcel delivery truck going to that area. A week later her brother was able to arrange a ride for us.

At about 4:45 one morning, Li Yi and I arrived at the backyard of the main post office, where many trucks were lined up to pick up parcels and mail. We waited in the cold until about 5:30, when Li Yi's brother came to us. "They're about to leave now," he said. We followed him to a truck parked by the exit gate. A few minutes later another young man appeared. He greeted Li Yi's brother and said, "Don't worry. Just leave it to me." Li Yi's brother left for work, and we sat beside the truck.

About twenty minutes later two other young men appeared. Li Yi's brother's friend told them, "These two girls are my cousins. If you will give them a ride, I will repay you with some good cigarettes." The two young men agreed to give us a ride. One of them climbed into the truck and opened the back of the canvas canopy. He told Li Yi's brother's friend, "Toss them up." I was too small even to reach the tailgate of the truck. Li Yi was taller, so she climbed into the truck by stepping on one of the back tires. Her brother's friend grabbed me by the waist and threw me to the young man standing in the truck, who caught me and dropped me into the back of the truck like a parcel. Before I could take a look around, the young man jumped down and closed the canopy.

Li Yi and I were in the dark. We called out to each other. I groped toward her voice. The first thing I touched was a parcel. The second thing was parcel, too. Then the truck began rolling through the city streets. Soon Li Yi and I got used to the darkness and were able to find each other.

"We are parcels now," I said to Li Yi.

"Yes," she replied, "except we have no address on our face."

I wanted to throw up because of the smell of the hot canopy and the lack of fresh air. Li Yi needed to relieve herself, but the drivers apparently had no intention of stopping. To distract ourselves from the physical discomfort, I suggested to Li Yi that we read the parcels to see where they had been sent from and where they were going. One parcel from Shandong Province was broken. The contents were big raw peanuts with pinkish skins. The discovery was exciting because our stomachs were empty. Li Yi started to eat some of the nuts, but I stopped her.

"Why can't I have some?" she asked.

"They will find out," I said. "It's like stealing."

"No, they won't. I mean, how could they?" Li Yi was upset.

"Only you and I are back here. They might think we opened the parcel deliberately."

"You are always trying to be good. You just want to be everyone's pet," Li Yi said. "I am going to eat these peanuts. I don't want to be a good girl anymore."

I was about to push her hand away from the parcel when the truck suddenly stopped. One of the drivers came around the back and opened the tent from the outside. "If you want to relieve yourselves, this is your only chance," he said without looking at us. Li Yi and I looked out. The truck had stopped in the barren, dusty countryside. The only cover was a field of desiccated corn. I was reluctant to go because the two young men would also go into the field.

Li Yi said, "Here is your chance to make a contribution to the agriculture of the country." Then she jumped off the truck. I followed her.

The two drivers were standing by the side of the truck, urinating into a ditch, as Li Yi and I walked into the field. We were worried the drivers would take off without us, so we only went a few rows into the field. When we came back to the truck, one of the drivers was searching for something among the parcels. His companion was leaning back against the truck, smoking. As we walked around to the back of the truck, the driver jumped down from the bed, holding the broken parcel of peanuts.

With the help of the drivers, we climbed back under the canopy. After driving for what seemed an entire day and night, the truck stopped again. One driver opened the canvas, saying, "Here you are. Get off. Get off." I asked the driver what time it was. He replied that it was six o'clock in the evening. Li Yi and I had been riding with parcels for twelve hours.

When the truck sped away, Li Yi and I realized that the drivers had dropped us off in the middle of the countryside. There were no houses, no animals, and no human beings around. Only more cornfields, stretching toward the mountains. I started crying. Li Yi told me to be quiet. She said that where there was a farm, there was a family. We walked for a mile or so and turned down a small road that led us to a peasant family farm. The only people home were a woman and a baby. We asked the woman if she knew if there was a Gan Xiao nearby. She said that there was one located on the mountain and that it would take us at least an hour to walk there.

After giving us some water to drink, the peasant woman led us through the fields to the foot of the mountain. When we arrived, she pointed to a path and said, "Stick to this path. At the end is the Gan Xiao, on the top of the mountain." We thanked her for her kindness and set off along the path. The sky was getting dark. I was nervous and said that I felt as if we were in a horrible movie and might wind up captured by bandits.

Li Yi shouted at me, "Be quiet. Do you want the Rebels to hear you? If no one can hear you, we are safe." The air was still, the mountain was quiet, but her voice echoed through the hills. I thought to myself, if there were any bandits lurking about, they knew where we were now. But I did not say a word. Li Yi's nervousness made me more scared.

The path was steep, and I kept telling myself after every turn that we would soon see the Gan Xiao. But turn after turn the Gan Xiao still did not appear. Soon the moon came out. With it appeared two iron gates and a soldier with a rifle on his shoulder.

"We've arrived. We've arrived," Li Yi and I shouted. We knew that this was the Gan Xiao even though there was no sign outside.

Standing before the soldier, we could see into the Gan Xiao well enough to make out people's faces. I could see some of my mother's colleagues walking by in the courtyard beyond the gates. The soldier would not let us in. Instead he asked us, "Who gave you permission to come here?"

We did not know how to respond. We had been taught to respect authority, and we were afraid.

"My mother is in there," I murmured.

"We came from Chengdu," Li Yi said, as though the name of the capital city bore some mystic power that would open the gates.

The soldier was not touched, replying, "Then go back there."

We did not know what we should do or what we could do. Li Yi and I were standing there, staring at the adults coming and going inside the courtyard, hoping we might see our parents. Finally someone recognized me. It was Uncle Cheng, one of my mother's close friends. He came to the gate and told the soldier, "I'll take care of these two."

Before I could say anything, Uncle Cheng led us away from the gate, saying, "I can get you into the Gan Xiao. There is a path up the back of the mountain. It is quite treacherous, but the bandits are not defending that path."[3] Uncle Cheng carried me and Li Yi followed, insisting she could walk. I did not understand what he meant by bandits, but I did know he was taking me to see my mother.

Riding on his back, I could see the moon hanging over the trees. It looked big and yellow, as though it were painted on a stage backdrop. I have never seen a moon like that again. I remembered telling Uncle Cheng that I wished the sun could be like that—so big and that pretty kind of yellow. Then I fell asleep under the slow sway of his walk.

I awoke to find myself in a single bed. I peaked out through mosquito netting: Another three single beds under mosquito nets were arranged along the wall, each with an enamel basin under it. On the other side of

---

3. During the Cultural Revolution, Jiang Qing approved eight different "model revolutionary dramas" for performance in China. One of these works, *Zhiqu Weihu Shan* (Conquering Fierce Tiger Mountain by Strategy), concerned a group of bandits who have established a stronghold at the top of a steep mountain. Members of the People's Liberation Army, the heroes, capture a bandit spy in town one day. From him they learn the secret password used to enter the stronghold. Picking a heroic PLA soldier, they send him up the mountain to infiltrate the bandit group. They plan to follow him up the mountain and attack the stronghold once he is in a position to let them inside.

Unbeknown to the PLA, the bandits have all of the passes into their territory guarded, making it impossible for the army to sneak up to the gates of the stronghold undetected. Luckily the soldiers meet a (politically reliable) hunter, who tells them, "I can take you into the bandits' stronghold. There is a path up the back of the mountain, but the bandits are not defending that pass because it is so treacherous, they don't think anyone can traverse it successfully." Unfortunately for the bandits, they have underestimated the heroic nature of the brave PLA soldiers, who overcome the obstacles of the path, enter the stronghold with the help of their infiltrator, and conquer the bandits.

Uncle Cheng's reference to bandits equates them with the soldiers running the Gan Xiao.

the room was a plain wood bench. A few tea mugs and rice bowls sat on a crude shelf above it. I wondered where Li Yi had gone and where the owners of the other beds were.

Suddenly I could hear voices, women approaching the door. It opened and four women came in, my mother third. As she approached me, the other three, now quiet, slipped under the mosquito nets into their beds. My mother raised the mosquito netting on the bed where I sat. She was holding a bowl of cracked corn. I looked at her, wanting to call her name, but I did not. Something about the way she looked at me and the silence of the other women told me that it was not time to speak. My mother looked at me for a moment without even smiling. No excitement. It was not much of a reunion after such a long separation.

"Here is your dinner," she said, handing me the bowl. "After you eat, go to sleep."

I ate the corn without speaking and tried to go to sleep, but I could not. The other women did not make a sound, no quiet chatting, not even the sound of their breathing.

My mother took a small folding chair out from under the bench, lit an oil lamp, and then turned out the overhead light. She began to write. I sat up in the darkness, watching her work silently. Writing away in the dim light of the oil lamp, my mother looked like a statue except for her hand moving across the page, page after page.

I wanted to talk to her, to touch her arm, to remind her I had come, but I did not. In our house, writing was a sacred activity. My brother and I were never allowed to disturb our parents while they were working. I remember thinking how important my mother's writing had to be that night for her to go without sleep. I got up to use the toilet, trying to attract her attention. She glanced at me for a second and then turned back to her writing.

Disappointed, I decided to look over her shoulder. I could see some of the words on the page: "Self-criticism," they said. Mom immediately turned the page upside down, concealing the words.

"You won't understand," she said, as she pushed me back to the bed.

I crawled back under the netting and sat up to watch as she returned to the bench. The word *self-criticism* kept going through my mind, helping me stay awake. I knew what self-criticism meant. It was the harshest form of punishment my parents leveled against their children. I remember having to write a self-criticism one time after my brother and I had got into trouble. We had been having a contest to see who could eat the most candy, and it made us both sick. I ran and hid, but my brother went to my parents. When he could no longer stand the bitterness of the medicine my mother gave him, he told them I had eaten the candy, too. My mother was so upset that I had made my brother sick that she made me write a self-criticism. When I was done, my father took the pages and locked them in his desk.

I never dreamed that there was someone so powerful that he or she could make my mother write self-criticism. My head was full of questions. Who was my mom writing her self-criticism for? Who was going to punish her? I could not answer the questions, so I promised myself that I would ask my mother when she came to bed.

She did not come to bed that night.

At dawn someone shook me awake and said, "Wake up. Wake up." I opened my eyes to see my mother's face. A military officer stood behind her. I knew he was an officer by the number of pockets on his jacket. Soldiers had only two pockets; officers had four.

"Tell Li *zhengwei* that you are leaving here today," said my mother.[4] I could not move my mouth. Mom demanded again, "Say it."

When I still made no sound, she said, "I'm sorry. This child can be very stubborn, but I will send her home today. I promise."

The political officer replied, "You had better see that she leaves. Don't forget your own problems. Otherwise ..."

My mother saw him to the door, apologizing all the way. Then she hurried over to me.

---

4. *Zhengwei* means "political commissar."

"It's not quite seven o'clock yet," said one of her roommates. "If you hurry, you can catch the bus that leaves at eleven o'clock."

I said that I wanted to leave with Li Yi because I had come with her.

"Forget Li Yi," my mother answered. "Mind your own business."

I tried everything I could to delay my departure. The later we left the Gan Xiao, the better chance I had of missing the bus and being able to stay another day.

At 7:30 the *zhengwei* returned. My mother gathered me up, and he escorted us to the gate. As we left, I gave the soldier on guard duty a nasty look. He did not seem to notice.

I followed my mother down the mountain. At the bus terminal my mother bought me a ticket and found that I still had an hour before the bus left. She took me to a small noodle shop and bought me a bowl of fried dumplings. Then she handed me a pair of chopsticks she had in her bag.

"I don't trust chopsticks in public places," she said. "I don't want you getting sick like your brother."

After I ate she took me back to the bus station. We were standing waiting for the bus when, without warning, she grabbed me by the arm and pulled my face close to hers. "Daughter, you must be obedient. Promise me."

I nodded to her even though I did not know what she meant by obedient or obedient to whom. Now I felt guilty. I was afraid that I had been disobedient for coming to visit my mother without anyone's permission.

The bus soon pulled up, and the passengers, all peasants, started to pile on, their baggage an assortment of bamboo boxes and baskets carrying everything from clothing to live chickens and ducks. Although I was from the city, I would not have been surprised to see someone try to carry a live pig onto the bus. The entire time they were boarding, the driver was cursing them for making his bus dirty.

Just as I was about to board the bus, my mother pulled a small package wrapped in rough paper from her bag: a half-kilo of crude brown sugar.

"Here," she said. "Your Uncle Cheng gave this to me. It's not very refined, so you will have to steam it before you give it to your brother. Take good care of it. Uncle Cheng's hepatitis is not so bad now, but this is all he had left."

The bus began to move before I found a seat. Looking out of the window, I could see my mother. I opened the window just in time to hear her shout, "Daughter, I'm sorry I let you down."

All the way home, and for weeks later, I wondered what she had meant. Why was she sorry, and how had she let me down? If she was sorry, why had she had to obey the *zhengwei* and send me home? And I was more uncertain than ever before. I wondered when my parents would come home or if I would ever even see them again.

♥♥

On December 22, 1968, China's youths got their marching orders when the *People's Daily* published Mao's latest instructions: "School graduates will be going to the countryside to get reeducated by the peasants." For most of China's youths, this was their final act in the Cultural Revolution. Some, imbued with Mao's ideology and the spirit of the times, volunteered to go to the remote areas. Others, those unfortunates whose parents did not have the political capital to protect them and who had no other alternatives, went because they were forced. All left to go to the poor, backward, remote areas to build the "new socialist countryside, marching to the song:

> *Go to the countryside,*
> *Go to the frontiers,*
> *To the places where the*
> *Motherland most needs you.*

For the Party, sending us to the countryside was a good strategic move. The Party could use our innocence and our knowledge to help push the countryside toward modernization. High morale is more economical than other kinds of material incentives. The Party was always skillful at manipulating the morale of youth. For some youths, going to the countryside was a chance to express their loyalty to the Party. For others, those whose parents had been denounced as bourgeois, it was a chance to escape the nightmare of the cities and offered the hope of being included in the collective again. However, it was refuge and restoration with a high price.

Going to the countryside started with canceling one's residence registration in the city. Households in China have a residence booklet in which all the family members are registered. The place of registry is based on one's birthplace. If a person happens to have been born in, say Shanghai, he cannot apply for residence in Beijing unless he gets a job in Beijing and his new employer is powerful enough to help him transfer his domicile from Shanghai to Beijing.

A child's domicile is usually registered with the parents. For example, if she was born in the countryside, she is a rural resident unless her parents are urban residents working for the government. By the same token, if she was born in the city but her parents are peasants, she is not eligible to apply for residence in the city. For urban citizens, the residence booklet is important because it is also used by the local government to allot food and cooking oil ration coupons.

When China's youths answered Mao's call to go to the countryside—either as loyal members of the Red Guards following Mao's directives or as victims of the Red Guards trying to escape the problems generated by their parents' Black status—those youths went to the local authority to remove their names from the family residence registers. Little did they know that they were sacrificing their urban domiciliary rights in the process.

In the center of Chengdu there is a statue of Chairman Mao, his right hand in the air, palm outstretched, his left hand behind his back. Around the time of the Shangshan-Xiaxiang (Go to the Countryside) Campaign, there was a popular joke that involved the statue. People would ask, "How long does Grandpa Mao expect us to stay in the countryside?"

One person would point to Mao's outstretched arm and say, "Five years."

Then another would point to the hand behind Mao's back and say, "No. He has four more fingers stretched out on that hand. Nine years." That joke came true for many unfortunates who spent at least a decade in the countryside.

From end of 1968, when Mao issued his call, to the beginning of 1972, some 4 million youths nationwide, myself among them, were sent to the countryside and to remote frontiers to build the new China. When I graduated from high school, I was sent to the countryside. I was seventeen years old. The bus ride from the city to the countryside took one entire day. At the edge of civilization, where the buses no longer traveled, I hitchhiked a ride on a tractor driven by an illiterate peasant. For several hours I rode in the constantly joggling tractor over rocky roads.

The tractor was a symbol of power for those who lived on China's agricultural communes. High social status accrued to drivers. The most important criterion for anyone who wanted to operate a tractor was political reliability. Knowing how to drive and knowing how a tractor worked did little to recommend someone to the cadres who ran the communes.

This driver knew that I was someone who was going to the countryside to be reeducated. I could see it in his eyes. I could tell that he was thinking, "Now it is my turn. I will teach this girl what the Cultural Revolution means."

When China's youths became rural residents, they discovered that they had to work the same long, hard hours as the peasants and for the same meager return. Only then did they realize how backward and primitive China really was. The second discovery, one more difficult to accept, was that regardless of how loyal they might be to Mao and to the Party, and regardless of how sympathetic they might be toward the peasants, even in the long run they were not going to reform the countryside of China. It was too huge a task even for all their young hearts and arms combined.

To begin with, the city-born-and-raised youths had neither the tools nor the experience for the job. The pens, posters, and debates they had used in their battles in the cities would not work in the countryside. The first task of a peasant is to feed himself and his family. The youths quickly realized that this would be their first need as well. All the idealistic fervor of the Red Guard units and the Propaganda Teams for Mao Zedong Thought faded under the relentless sun and endless fields of wheat and rice. In the face of such a tough reality, Mao's once-powerful ideology seemed vapid.

Many of these unfortunates wound up staying in the countryside for more than ten years before they finally managed to get back to the city. Many more were unable to become urban citizens again even after the end of the Cultural Revolution in 1976. Some lost hope of returning to their urban lives and stayed, marrying peasants to survive the hardships and trying to make a life for themselves in the remote areas. Other youths died in the countryside, lost to their parents, becoming lonely rural ghosts. The 1970s quietly watched countless families become empty nests, their foundations crumbling.

Ten years after the Cultural Revolution began, it began to wind to a close with Mao's death in September 1976. It was officially called to an end when the Party cracked down on the Gang of Four less than a month later. During the Cultural Revolution, so many were killed, so many were wounded, and far more were distorted under the same ideological slogans. The Revolution was a giant burning furnace that fired our souls and our dreams but left only dust when the fire burned down.

THE STORIES

PRISONERS AND
WARDENS

O*n the June day I went to interview Xiaoyu, the dust in the hot Beijing air clouded the blue in the sky. The weather reminded me of a southern California Santa Ana Indian summer, when the hot, dry winds blow off the desert. Riding on my bicycle against the wind, I spent more than an hour getting to her house.*

Xiaoyu is a technician at a hospital, and she lives with her husband, a writer, in an apartment provided by her husband's work unit, the Ministry of Culture. When I knocked at the door, it was opened by a tiny, pale woman dressed in a too-large blue dress that seemed to intensify her diminutive frame.

During the interview, she sewed, making a shirt for her nephew from a piece of red-print cloth. She told me that she went to work every day, riding her bicycle for an hour and a half, not because there were experiments at the hospital that she had to perform and not because she felt a sense of social responsibility, but simply "because it's my job."

When she talked, she frowned slightly, scrunching her eyebrows together when she got to the difficult-to-tell parts of her story, her gold, wire-framed glasses slipping down her nose. She appeared tense and mildly depressed even though her tone was clear and calm. Her voice, like her body, had a girlish charm.

I was the baby of our family. I had four older brothers named Xiaogang, Xiaojiang, Xiaobin, and Xiaonan. My oldest brother, Xiaogang, was a freshman at the Number Two University of Foreign Languages in

Beijing. Xiaojiang lived near Xiaogang, in a Beijing boarding school. My two youngest brothers lived at home.

Prior to the Cultural Revolution, my father was a highly placed official in the Ministry of Public Security. We lived in a remote suburb some one hundred li [approximately thirty miles] from Beijing, close to the H jail for important political criminals. I frequently watched the prisoners fetching water from the boiler room or laboring in the courtyard.

We were reasonably well-off in those days, with a maid in the family to cook and clean the house for us. A chauffeur drove me to school every day. I was constantly spoiled by everyone in my family. I lived in a child's paradise. I never knew how different my family was until the day my oldest brother was arrested one winter Saturday in 1966.

On the day we learned of his arrest, my mother had come home earlier than usual to help the maid prepare a special dinner for Xiaogang's birthday. Once the dinner was ready and the square table set, we sat down to wait for him to arrive. We waited and waited. The dinner got cold. The maid warmed it up. We began to get worried. Dinner got cold again. It was warmed up again. By now my mother could not cover her anxiety. She kept walking out of the house, expecting to see my brother coming down the road. When the clock standing by the front door struck nine, my father said, "Maybe he isn't coming home. Perhaps we should start eating."

Just as we were about to begin, the front door opened and my second brother rushed inside, slamming the door. My mother ran to his side and asked him where Xiaogang was. Very much out of breath, he told us that Xiaogang had been arrested. Keeping his voice level, my father handed Xiaojiang a glass of water and asked him what had happened.

Xiaojiang answered, "I went to my brother's dormitory late yesterday afternoon to ask him to come home today. That's what mother asked me to do. When I got there, his room was a disaster. It looked like someone had turned it inside out. He was not in the room; neither was his roommate. I had no idea what had happened, but my intuition told me that it was trouble. On my way to the dormitory phone to call home, Li Geng, Xiaogang's roommate, stopped me and told me what happened. He told me that some counterrevolutionary graffiti had appeared on the campus and that Xiaogang had been arrested for the crime."

Xiaojiang learned that Xiaogang was being held in the Beijing Municipal Public Security Bureau. My brother told Li Geng that Xiaogang would be fine as long as they took him to the Security Bureau, which was controlled by my father's ministry. Li Geng suggested that my brother was a primary suspect because of my father's political problems and that it might not be wise to call home.

Xiaojiang continued, "Li Geng told me to go home and tell you what happened. I left the dormitory and hid in the city. If the situation was really as bad as it seemed, I didn't want to be followed. At three o'clock this morning I started walking home."

My father asked the maid to bring a basin of hot water so my brother could soak his feet. He had walked more than sixty kilometers that day. Despite his safe arrival, Xiaojiang was still wrought up. In his right hand he still grasped the brick that he had carried against potential attack while he walked through the dark.

What none of us had known before learning of my elder brother's arrest was that my father had been put under house arrest by revolutionary Rebels in his department. He had lost his right to speak in public and his influence on the Beijing Municipal Public Security Bureau. Before my father could do anything to free Xiaogang, he was charged with crimes against the state and, without a court hearing or trial, was transferred to the H jail. This was just the first of a string of arrests on similar charges. Following the path walked by my eldest brother were my father's older brother, then my mother's brother, then my mother's sister-in-law (who was Russian and a Revolutionary Party member), and finally my father.

Four or five days after Xiaogang's arrest, I heard a friend talking to my father. He said that the revolutionary Rebels would search our house the next day. They wanted to find some "written evidence" they could use against my father so he could be executed for counterrevolutionary activities. That night I could not fall asleep. I did not know if my father had anything that could be used as written evidence. I knew that I had a lot of children's books that had been bought for me by my father. He liked to give me books as a reward for good grades in school and as birthday and New Year presents. I imagined that the Rebels would find those books and use them as evidence against my father. I got up, gathered up the books, and stole into the courtyard, where I ran into Xiaojiang and Xiaonan.

"What are you doing here?" Xiaojiang asked.

"What are you doing here?" I asked back.

"You tell us first," Xiaonan said, adding, "or else I won't help you with your math anymore." I hated math and would never have had decent scores on my math exams without his help, so I surrendered.

"I want to bury my books. Will you help me dig a hole, please?"

He agreed and told me they wanted to bury their hunting rifles and bullets. While they dug a hole under an apple tree, I helped them put wax on their bullets and remove parts from their rifles. We buried our treasures and our dreams there. Years later my brothers and I went back to where our house had been, thinking we might recover our treasures. Where our house and orchard had been a number of new buildings were under construction. There were a few trees still standing, but there was no way we could tell which might be the one we sought, and we returned to the city. Maybe it was better to not dig up the secrets of our childhood, better to let the nightmares of the past remain buried.

One afternoon shortly after my uncle's arrest, the Rebels came to throw us out of our house. With the exception of a few personal clothes and toilet articles, all of our belongings and household goods were sealed in the house. A short, bony man, who used to be one of my father's subordinates, was now the head of the Rebels. He shouted at my father, "You must plead guilty in front of the revolutionary masses. Otherwise you put yourself on the road to ruin." I wondered how such a small man had this much power. Why was he allowed to shout at my father? I thought he must be some kind of dangerous demon.

Our whole family was driven to a military academy in Beijing. This made it more convenient for the Rebels to interrogate my parents. It also would allow them to turn my parents over to the revolutionary citizens' committees for public criticism and denunciation.

At the academy, our family was housed on the first floor of an H-shaped building. Where we had previously enjoyed an entire house, we now had to live in two rooms, one for my parents and one for my two younger brothers and myself. There was no lavatory or kitchen. We used the public facilities of the military. My mother had to go alone to the canteen to buy our food. The first time she sent me, the children of the military spit in my face and shouted abuse at me. She never even tried to send my brothers for fear that they would only get in trouble by fighting with the other children. But she didn't find it easy to go either. One morning after she came home with breakfast, I noticed that she was covered with mud and dirt thrown by the rebellious children. Every time the children saw us, they would bare their teeth at us and shout, "*Da doo*" [Down with] ..." If they got a response or thought we looked scared, they would continue to shout, "*Da doo*" and add my father's name. My brothers would have gladly sought revenge had my mother not restrained them. She didn't want to stir up any more trouble. She knew that our actions would only bring more misery down on my father's head.

Every morning after breakfast my mother sent us out of the apartment and away from the academy. She didn't care where we went. She just wanted us out of the sight of the Rebels. In those days counterrevolutionary slogans were often scrawled on the walls somewhere in the academy. My mother did not want any of her other children thrown into jail.

One morning around seven o'clock, before my mother sent us from the apartment, I went to a public lavatory. On the wall in the lavatory were the characters for the words *Chairman Mao* written upside down, with an *X* drawn through them.[1] When I saw this, I ran home immediately and told my mother. While she was frightened, she also knew that if she reported the incident to the Rebels, they might be a bit easier on my father. However, I was frightened that the Rebels might think I had written the characters on the wall. I wrapped my arms around my mother's legs and begged her not to report the writing. She then asked me if anyone had seen me in the lavatory or along the path. When I assured her that no one had been around, she relented. Worried that we might get blamed anyway, she rushed us out of the apartment, saying, "Hurry and get out before those rats smell something and try to start more trouble."

The slogan went undiscovered until noon. Once they found the writing, the Rebels gathered up everyone they could find who had been near the lavatories that morning. When they came to our house, my mother told them that we could not be responsible. She had sent us to the city early that morning before the "reactionary event" had taken place.

For all the necessity of the visit, the lavatories were scary places to go. You never knew when you would be set upon and cursed by the Rebels or their children. Since the most dangerous times were at night, my mother had a house rule forbidding us to go to the lavatory unless we absolutely had to. Every night after dinner she would place a bucket in our room so we could urinate, and then she would lock us in where we would be safe. This arrangement didn't bother my brothers; they were teenagers and not modest at all. I was much too shy to use the bucket, however. My solution to the problem was not to drink any liquids or eat any soup at dinner. In this manner I was usually able to wait until morning to use the toilet.

One midnight I was awakened by a noisy, upset stomach. I tried to ignore it. I lay on my back, then on my left side, then on my right side, and then on my stomach. Soon my stomach hurt so much that I was

---

1. This suggests that Chairman Mao should be done away with.

wet with sweat. I woke up my brothers, and they suggested that I climb out the window. We didn't want to tell my mother because she would be worried.

Although it was midwinter, I climbed out of the window in my nightgown. It was no protection from the cold. I ran as fast as I could toward the lavatory, about four hundred meters from the apartment. I was almost there when I saw another person headed in the same direction. I quickly lay down behind a small pile of bricks. I didn't want to be seen by the wrong people. They would report me, and I might be accused of writing the counterrevolutionary slogans. I peeked over the top of the bricks, trying to see who was there. It was the daughter of one of the Rebels.

Once a little bad luck finds you, more soon follows. I stayed on the cold ground behind the bricks, hoping she would not be long. My hands and feet were numb with the cold, and I was frightened that she would hear my teeth chattering. She was not in a hurry to finish her business. I began to imagine that she had seen me and was waiting in the lavatory to catch me and report me to the authorities. I tried to hang on, but my body wouldn't wait. I lost control of my bowels. Now I was in real trouble. I couldn't go into the lavatory for fear of being discovered, and I couldn't return home because I was too embarrassed. Fortunately for me, Xiaobin was worried about me and had come to look for me. He picked me up and carried me home. We did not tell my mother about what happened.

My father was labeled the biggest *zouzipai* in the public security and court bureaucracy. [2] Every time he was denounced at a public meeting, my mother was sent to accompany him to the denunciation.

My mother was a reticent person. She had to be because of her position as a director of the General Office of the Ministry of Public Security. She was in charge of the top-secret documents section. The Rebels tried to get her to testify against my father. She just kept her mouth

---

2. *Zouzipai* means "capitalist roader."

shut firmly. When this failed, they tried to force her to divorce my father. She steadfastly refused this as well. One morning she failed to return from her meeting with the Rebels. No one, not even my father, was able to find out where she was taken.

When the Rebels were unable to find sufficient evidence of my father's counterrevolutionary activities to have him executed, they exiled him to a camp in northeast China. My brothers and I were not told of his transfer. For many weeks we lived in those two rooms, wondering if either of our parents was still alive. One day my brother told me he had overheard two Rebels talking about our mother. He learned that she was to be denounced the next day at a meeting called the Hundred Thousand People's Meeting. My brothers and I went to the meeting, which was held in the Workers' Sports Arena in Beijing. On the platform I saw my mother standing along with other thought criminals. Hung around her neck on a piece of thin wire was a large iron sign that read, "I am the cursed wife of *XX*." Her neck was bowed by the heavy sign, and the wire was visibly cutting into her neck. Her head was splotched with bald spots.

The Rebels forced her to a microphone at the center of the stage. They commanded her to publicly state her guilt. She refused. One of the Rebels kicked her in the knee. She lost her balance and fell down on the platform. The leader of the Rebels stepped on her back and shouted, "You are dead! You are dead!!" My brother and I could not bear to watch, and we ran from the meeting.

We didn't hear anything from my mother and father for about a year after the meeting. People told us that they were forbidden to write to anyone. One spring day a little boy told me that my mother had returned to the city but that she was still forbidden to go home. He was the son of one of the Rebels, and he had overheard his father talking at the dinner table. He said he could take me to see my mother.

The next day he came for me. We traveled across the academy compound, through several buildings, until we came to the southernmost part of the camp. We entered a deserted building, filled with broken furniture and cast-off household goods. He took me to a window that faced out of the compound and told me to watch for the workers while he stood guard at the door.

Through the window I could see a huge field. Several dozen people were laboring there, planting the land without talking, singing, or laughing. The scene reminded me of a concentration camp I once saw in a movie. Everyone in the field looked old and exhausted. I looked at them carefully. A weary, thin woman caught my eye. The way she moved reminded me of my mother. I was about to take another more careful look when the boy pulled me from the window. "Let's get out of here. Someone is coming."

Once we were clear of the building, I asked my guide if he was sure that my mother was working in the field.

"Definitely," the boy answered. "You mean you didn't see her? What a pity! We can try next week if you are not afraid. Women prisoners do reform through labor there every Thursday under the surveillance of the Rebels."

I was upset that I had to wait for a week, not knowing whether I would see my mother or not. Since it was my day to use the showers, I decided to take mine early and try to wash away my blues. I went to the public bathhouse, hoping that I would not have to share a shower. Usually three or four people would have to use a single stall. I undressed and walked to a stall in a remote corner where I could have some privacy.

I was standing under the shower rinsing my hair when I noticed a pair of feet standing in the stall with me. I froze, with my hands on the top of my head, wondering who had joined me and why. Then I noticed that the feet looked familiar. They were my mother's feet. I could recognize them from the way her small toes curled under the big toe on her right foot.

Slowly I raised my eyes to the woman's face. It was my mother! I almost collapsed. I couldn't refrain from saying "Mama" in a little voice. She put her index finger across my mouth in response. Then she turned my back to her. She started rubbing my back and shoulders with her hands. Her hands were so rough, but her touch was light. Nevertheless, my back was on fire from the pain and love in that touch. She did not say anything.

As we dressed after the shower, a few people in the room criticized her with their looks. Others showed their sympathy but were afraid to say anything in her support. When we were finished dressing, my mother pointed to the door, meaning that I should leave first without her. I took her hint and left, but I did not head home. I hid behind a tree to watch my mother as she left.

Sitting in front of the bathhouse was a pretty woman who looked familiar. She appeared to be in her early thirties, with an athletic figure, fair skin, and a delicate mouth. Suddenly I recognized her. I knew her from my father's office. She had been one of the arraignment secretaries and had been nice to me when I visited the ministry.

I was about to come out of my hiding place and find out what she was doing there when my mother walked out of the bathhouse. She looked around a bit as though she was trying to find me, but I remained hidden behind the tree. I knew she was not allowed to see or talk to anyone, especially a family member. I didn't want to give the Rebels any reason to give my mother more trouble.

From behind the tree, I could hear the pretty woman yelling at my mother, "Don't move. Hands up." I peeked around the tree to see her search my mother roughly. When she didn't find anything, she shouted; "What are you looking around for? Move!"

My mother lowered her head and moved away, the woman following her. That was the last time I saw my mother alive. She died in 1976, just before the Gang of Four was brought to justice. She was fifty-two years old.

I often wonder why I didn't ask my mother anything about herself when we were in the shower. I wonder why I didn't talk to her much during her life. Why had I let her reticence keep me from knowing her? Now it is too late.

Five years after she died, the Ministry of Public Security gave a memorial in my mother's honor. The memorial speech declared that my mother had been a Communist Party member par excellence. My brothers and I were unmoved. Such abstract honors would not bring her back to life, nor could they atone for the pain and agony she needlessly suffered. At the memorial meeting, her former captors tried to shake our hands. Like my two surviving brothers, I stood motionless, staring at them with my hands clasped behind my back. I will never forgive them.

BUTTERFLIES
AND RAIN

I *first met Linbin in the office of his uncle, an official in the Ministry of Culture, whom I interviewed in 1983 while I was a reporter with the Xinhua News Agency. Linbin's dark eyes and red cheeks make him look like a cute boy. If he had not been smoking and had shaved more carefully, the image would have been complete.*

Linbin is known locally for his calligraphy. The practice of writing with a brush is one of the spiritual qualities and habits of the traditional Chinese scholar. Such practices have largely disappeared among the younger generation, surviving only as a hobby.

He works as an editor for a literature magazine published in Guangzhou. When I began talking to my friends for this book, I called Linbin for an interview. We made arrangements to meet in Shenzhen in June. I arrived in town a day late and learned that he had gone to Beijing. I figured that I would probably run into him when I was there later in the month. One afternoon a few days after I arrived in the capital city, he walked unannounced into my hotel room carrying a watermelon. "Damn," he said. "It's too hot." He dropped into a chair by the window and then knocked the melon against the edge of the coffee table to split it open. "Sorry, I don't have a knife," he explained. "Besides, we're old friends."

He sat with a cigarette in one hand and a piece of melon in the other as we talked.

"No wonder you're still a bachelor," I teased him.

"Ha! That's what you think. I'm going to get married," he replied.

He told me that his future wife was a medical student in Beijing. "I'm not marrying her out of love," he said. "I don't believe in love anymore. I used to love my mother and my father and my grandfather. My parents used to love the Party. Look where it got us. My parents gave up everything and tried to become wu chan zhe.[1] *I want to be you* chan zhe,[2] *and damn, it's much more difficult than the other way around. It's not easy because I can still hear my mother lecturing me about how a youth should establish high spiritual goals."*

It was raining. Very heavy. My brother Linguang and I were on a journey looking for my mother. I was nine and he was ten. We had not seen our parents for two years. My father had been the mayor of our town but was expelled from his position by the Rebels as the "biggest capitalist roader" in 1967. He was sent to a coal mine for reform through labor. My mother had been the director of the municipal hospital but was imprisoned in the same year, accused of being a subversive.

Both my parents came from rich and prestigious families in southern China. When my father was young, he had six personal maids. In the 1930s, as a teenager he gave up his luxurious lifestyle and devoted himself to the Communist Party.

My mother was the daughter of a major general in the Investigation and Statistics Bureau of the Military Commission, the ISBMC.[3] When she met my father, she was a student in a local Christian school. My father was in the underground movement and happened to come to her school looking for converts to communism. Mother fell in love with him.

One day my mother disappeared from home. Her father, Waigong (mother's father), sensed that she was with my father and that they were about to leave for the north, the center of the communists. My father's name was on the ISBMC's list of suspected communist agents.

---

1. *Wu chan zhe* are people without property, proletarians.
2. *You chan zhe* is a person of property.
3. The ISBMC was the notorious intelligence agency of the KMT.

Waigong imposed a curfew on the city and sent out the Xian Bin [the KMT military police] to search for my mother. They searched three days in vain. He then told my mother's mother that "the second daughter has gone on a long journey, and she will not come home for a long long time."

Waigong was arrested at home in 1949 when the Communist Party took over the city. Shortly thereafter he was sent to the Fushun prisoner-of-war camp in northeast China.

My father and mother were assigned to work in Hubin, their home city, by the Party. When the Cultural Revolution began, the Party launched a witch-hunt and gathered in my parents because of their parents' positions. No thought was given to their loyalty to the Party or to their contributions to the Party and Chinese society.

My mother was a sensitive and caring person. She was fond of saying that she did not care about a person's political fortunes. She was a doctor, and anyone who was sick could be her patient. One summer afternoon in 1967, as the fire of the Cultural Revolution was being sparked in the city, three stout men walked into my mother's office. They asked her to come with them to see a patient. This was not particularly extraordinary. While common people came to the doctor's office when they were ill, those with more social position frequently called a doctor to their homes when they did not feel good. What was different was that the three men refused to tell my mother who and where was the patient, and they covered her eyes with a blindfold.

The three men took Mother to a house just outside the city. In the house was an old man lying in a bed. When she saw him, Mother said that he looked familiar, like someone wanted by the government. No one responded, but the house was all of a sudden full of tension.

Later, when she arrived home, Mother told Father that she strongly suspected the old man was He Ying [Black Eagle], a former head of the local bandit group. In the late 1940s, the Communist Party sent an armed force into Hubin to suppress the local bandits. My father and mother had been among that force. At the time of the suppression, the Party had offered a large reward for bringing He Ying to justice, but he managed to escape them. Father warned Mother to keep her mouth shut and her eyes closed. He was afraid that Mother had accidentally been witness to a conspiracy of the Party and that she could be in big trouble.

He was right. We never figured out what happened, but she had become a threat to someone. That evening Mother walked into the bedroom I shared with Linguang. She told us that she and my father would be going on a long journey and might not come home for a long time. She told us that we had to look after each other.

The next day was Sunday. Mother took Linguang and me to the biggest department store in the city. She bought a new schoolbag for each of us. Then we went to a fancy restaurant. This was all strange to me. I asked Mother why we did not go home to have dinner with Father. She said Father had something important to do for their long journey, and he did not want any distractions.

After dinner, instead of going back home, she took brother Linguang and me to Yeye's [paternal grandfather's] house. Mother sent us to play with our cousin when she talked to Yeye. In a while we were called into the living room. My mother was sobbing. I had never seen her cry before, and it frightened me. She stood up from the chair, pulled Linguang and me under her arms, and said, "Study conscientiously." Only these two words. Then she walked out of the house.

It took me a long time to learn that my mother had been imprisoned for crimes against the state. While we lived with Yeye, Linguang and I attended a nearby school. For the first couple of weeks, kids at school were friendly. This did not last long. Soon we began to hear *ye zhong*.[4] Kids shouted it at us wherever we went. We sought protection from Yeye, but he was little help.

Yeye had a wife whom we called Nainai [father's mother]. Nainai did not like us. She preferred our cousin because his parents were members

---

4. *Ye zhong* figuratively means "bastard;" literally, "wild seed." The word implies a person does not know his or her mother or father.

of the People's Liberation Army, and therefore they were good people. My father and mother were bad people. Nainai would repeat this to us whenever we had a quarrel with our cousin. Yeye showed a little bit of sympathy for us. Nainai so disliked us that she would not even allow us to eat until our cousin was finished with his breakfast. She did not feed us enough for lunch or dinner either. After each meal she locked up the kitchen.

One day I was fighting with my cousin. He wanted the cup I was using to drink water, and I refused to give it to him. He punched me in the face, and I punched him back. My cousin was much bigger than I. When Linguang joined the fight to help protect me, my cousin started screaming, "Nainai, save me! Save me! The brothers are beating me." Nainai dashed out of her room with a rod in her hand. Without asking what was going on, she began to beat Linguang from head to toes. I tried to drag her away, but I couldn't; I was too small. Linguang was lying on the ground with cuts and bruises all over his body. Nainai locked him in the attic that night. The next day was Sunday. While Nainai was gone to the market, I searched the house for the key to the attic. I climbed the ladder to reach the door and freed my brother. He walked into the bedroom, put some clothes in his schoolbag, and ran out the house. I ran outside and shouted, "Where are you going?"

"To look for Mom," he answered. I ran after him, begging him to take me with him. Without stopping he shouted, "You go back. Don't come with me." But I did not stop. Suddenly a loud crash of thunder rolled over in the sky. Linguang stopped running, too startled by the noise to move, and waited for me.

We had only a vague idea where Mother was. The only thing we knew was that she was in a prison in Hubin. And the city was faraway from Yeye's house. We would have to take a train to get there, and we had no money. Linguang said we should go to a mountain village where they grew peaches. It was harvest time, and we could make some small money picking up the peach pits everyone would be spitting on the ground. We could sell them to herbalists, who used the pits for making traditional Chinese medicines.

The rain had stopped as we arrived at the village. Linguang told me to begin collecting the pits while he went to get some bamboo. He was afraid that Nainai would come after us. He planned to sharpen some bamboo poles to use to chase her off if she showed up. I began to collect the pits, but before long, I began to feel hungry. I told Linguang, who noticed a nearby tomato plot. Even though all the tomatoes were green, we began to eat a few. Even now I still remember the stinging taste of those green tomatoes. No sooner had I bit into one than a boy about my age, wearing only a pair of shabby shorts, appeared in front us. He asked where we came from and why we did not go home to eat. I burst out crying. I was scared. Linguang told the boy we were orphans.

Instead of chasing us off, he took us to a straw hut he said was his home. The hut was dark and dirty. A man was smoking in the hut. The boy called him Dad. The man was skinny and weather-beaten. He did not ask us any questions. He cooked something for us. I do not remember what kind of food we ate. I just remember eating as the sky turned cloudy. The boy's father said that it was going to rain again. He urged Linguang and me to go home so that our parents wouldn't be worried about us. Then he took a straw hat off a hook on the wall and gave it to me. It appeared to be the only hat in the hut. I took off the navy blue striped shirt I was wearing and gave it to the boy.

Linguang changed his mind. He decided we should sneak onto the train and keep the peach pits as food. Lightning flashed in the sky, while the thunder rolled overhead. We ran through the rain toward the station, my brother ahead of me. We had to cross a 200-meter-long wooden bridge. In the middle of the bridge, the wind blew stronger. It grabbed the hat from my head. I stopped running to watch the hat swirling against the sky and then disappearing with the rain into the river. I was sad. It was like a part of my life was gone with the hat. Linguang stopped and screamed for me to hurry up.

We ran all the way to the station with our heads bent over to avoid the rain beating our faces. As we ducked into the entrance, there was Yeye. I stole a glance at Yeye, who looked back evenly. I made eye contact with Linguang, who looked disappointed. Yeye started talking. He said it was all right if we wanted to go, but not to leave like this. He gave us some money for the train ticket. The last thing he said to us was, "Be good human beings like your mother."

The train took a day and two nights getting to the city. Once we were off the train, Linguang and I decided that the municipal hospital where Mother used to be chief resident was our first stop. We thought we might get some information about where Mother was jailed. In order to get to the downtown area where the hospital was located, we needed to pass through a city wall with a gate. We walked and walked. The road was muddy from the rain. Just at the foot of the gate there was a crowd.

Children are always curious, no matter if they are happy or sad. Linguang and I were just children then. We squeezed into the crowd. At the front, just to one side of the gate, there was a dead body wrapped in a straw mat. The straw mat was not long enough, and the person's calves stuck out one end and the head out the other. A thumb-thick thread was tied around the person's neck, and the face was covered with an old rag. The people in the crowd were saying, "Poor woman" sympathetically.

One woman wondered aloud if the dead woman had any family members. She told us that the body had been lying there for four days. I took another look at the body, and I noticed that the calves and feet were swollen. A man in the crowd said he was told by some other people that the person was a woman. Supposedly she had a husband and children, but the Rebels who had dumped the body there had not informed them of the woman's death.

Linguang dragged me out of the crowd. He said we had work to do getting our mother out of jail. He reminded me of the heroes in patriotic movies where Communist Party members were put into the KMT's jail and then bailed out by rich communist sympathizers. We slipped through the gate without being noticed, and about twenty minutes later we found ourselves standing outside the hospital. Suddenly I heard a woman calling my nickname, "Bin Bin." It was Aunt Wu, who had been my mother's best friend.

"Why are you kids here?" Aunt Wu asked.

"Where is my mother?" I asked her.

"She's not here," Aunt Wu answered. "Come with me." She took the two of us to her house and cooked a bowl of noodles and eggs for us. Linguang refused to eat the noodles until she told us where our mother was. I followed his example and put down my chopsticks, even though I was hungry. Aunt Wu paused for a few seconds and then said, "Okay, you will know sooner or later anyway."

"Which city gate did you come through?" Aunt Wu looked at us.

"The southern gate," Linguang said.

"So you saw it already," she paused again.

"What? What did we see already?" I asked quietly.

"The dead body. That is your mother. The Rebels said that she had alienated herself from the people and the Party. They say she committed suicide." Aunt Wu starting crying.

Linguang did not cry. Neither did I. A silence veiled the house. Aunt Wu was frightened by our lack of reaction and shouted, "Say something, boys; I beg you, say something!" while shaking our shoulders.

Linguang seemed to grow up immediately. He moved Aunt Wu's hands off his shoulders and said, "I will get revenge."

"We will get revenge," I echoed.

Linguang said he was going to take Mother home. Aunt Wu told us the Rebels had decided to leave mother's body outside the gate for ten days as a warning to other capitalist roaders: this would be the end for anyone who refused to cooperate with the Rebels. Aunt Wu agreed that we should reclaim Mother's body, but she suggested we should wait to act until after dark.

We stayed at Aunt Wu's house the whole afternoon. The clock on the wall seemed to tick away the time slowly. By eight o'clock, the darkness was complete. To be safe we waited another hour before the two of us walked out of the house and headed across town. Aunt Wu did not come along.

At the southern gate, we discovered that the crowd had disappeared. That was fine with us, but Mother's body had disappeared, too. Thinking there might have been some good-hearted people who hid Mother somewhere nearby to protect her from the rain and sun, we looked through the bushes for several hours without luck. She was gone.

Three days later Aunt Wu came home with some information. Because the corpse was decomposing, the Rebels had buried Mother outside the walls in a village called the Lotus Flower. Linguang and I left for the village immediately. It didn't take us long to find Mother's grave. The Rebels had buried my mother just under the surface of the earth. The rain had already brushed much of the earth away, and we could now see her face. Looking at the body, I could not believe that this was my mother. I wanted to talk to her. I wanted her to hold me and tickle me again. I kept calling, "Mom, Mom—do you hear me?" but there was no return voice to say, "Don't be afraid, Bin Bin. Mom is here," like she had when I was frightened. I started crying. It began to rain again.

Following a clash of thunder came a man's voice: "Oh, boys, you are here." It was Jue Shu [Crippled Uncle] who lived in the Lotus Flower village. He was not a family relative. We knew him because he knew our mother, who had treated him at the hospital. Looking down at Mother, he said, "Your mother was a good human being."

Without thinking twice I kneeled down in front of him. "Help us, Jue Shu, please. We have to take Mother home."

"Don't act like a silly child," Jue Shu pulled me up. "You cannot take your mother home. She's dead. The best thing we can do is to bury her properly."

"All right—but we need a place with good *feng shui*," my brother added.[5]

"I know a place on my land surrounded by peach trees," Jue Shu said, "and the *feng shui xian sheng* [a geomancer] in the village said the location is very good."

Jue Shu went down the mountain to get a shovel. Linguang took off his shirt and began to wipe the blood off Mother's face. Then he cov-

---

5. *Feng shui* literally means "wind and water." The term refers to a place where the soul can be at peace.

ered her upper body with his shirt. I wrapped the shirt I was wearing around Mother's legs.

Shortly Jue Shu came back with a shovel, an old but clean bedsheet, a basin, a towel, and a jar of salts. He filled the basin with rainwater and put the salts in it. As he cleaned my mother's body, he explained that the salts would keep the body from decomposing. After he finished his work, he wrapped the body with the sheet. Then we carried my mother to Jue Shu's property.

We did not leave any earth raised over the gravesite. Jue Shu said such a grave would arouse suspicions. We did have one way of locating the grave again: a willow tree. Standing in front of the willow tree, Jue Shu said, "Forgive me, Doctor Chen. When all this passes, we will build a nice home for you." Then he demanded that my brother and I kneel down and promise Mother, "We will be good human beings." As we spoke our last promises, the rain stopped. A butterfly appeared and flew lightly around the willow tree for a few seconds. Then it disappeared into the bushes as suddenly as it appeared. Jue Shu assured us that Mother had heard us and was content.

Jue Shu said that the butterfly was the incarnation of Mother, whose soul was now riding on the butterfly's wings on its way to heaven. I did not believe him. I thought Jue Shu was superstitious. However, it was mysterious to see the butterfly wheeling around the willow tree.[6]

Four years later our father was pronounced "politically clear" and allowed to leave the coal mine. The three of us, my father, my brother, and I, went to Lotus Flower village to thank Jue Shu. But when we got to the village, we were told that he had died and no one knew when or how or where he was buried. We found the willow tree and Mother's grave. I felt like she was smiling in her sleep, undisturbed since we had laid her there. My father was completely lost in his sorrow. We placed a tablet on the grave that said, "The grave of Mother Linting." That was

---

6. In Chinese mythology, the butterfly signifies that if two people cannot be together in this life, they will be together in the next.

the name she used at her parents' home before she ran away with my father. This would protect her because only those who loved her would recognize this name.

In 1979 the Party decided to announce Mother's rehabilitation. They reversed their verdict of *jieji yiji fenzi* [alien-class element], which had been imposed on her more than ten years before. Two Party officials from the hospital where my mother had worked came to our house one afternoon. These officials said that they understood how painful and sad we all felt about Mother's death. But, once dead, no one could bring Mother back to life. Their advice to my father was that he should look to the future and believe in the Party, which still cared for its sons and daughters. They said that denouncing my mother as *jieji yiji fenzi* had served the needs of the Party in those years. Announcing her rehabilitation now also served the needs of the Party. Their parting words announced a memorial meeting, to be held the following week.

I hid in another room while this conversation was taking place. I knew that the pair were part of the group that had put my mother in prison originally. I felt the endless dark. How could these people still be in power? How could they possibly come to Father without any shame or guilt whatsoever? When I asked these questions of my father, he could only shake his head. He was too angry and too saddened to say anything. There was a voice at the bottom of my heart telling me that I had to do something at the memorial meeting.

In these meetings, in order to show their newfound sympathy and understanding, the officials would routinely ask the dead person's family if they had any requests to present to the Party. Usually this meant the family had some hand in planning the meeting or could ask for some compensation for their loss. I had an idea that would embarrass and shame these hooligans. I told Father the idea, and he agreed to go along with my plan.

It was a peculiar memorial meeting. There was no coffin, no body, and no urn for the memorialized person's ashes. The only note of my mother's presence was a picture of her, chosen by me from the few remaining photos of her, hung in the center of the meeting hall. It had been taken in the 1950s, when she was bursting with youthful vigor and wore an innocent smile. That beautiful face seemed to have nothing to do with the death.

I chose this picture for many reasons. The most important one was Waigong, who attended the meeting. The last time he had seen his favorite daughter was the day before she ran off with my father to join the Communist Party forty years ago. When Mother reappeared in her home city as a doctor, Waigong was serving his days in the prison camp controlled by the Party. When Waigong was released and finally allowed to come home, my mother had been put into prison by the same Party to whom she had dedicated her whole life. The daughter in Waigong's memory was that lovely, indulgent, charming young lady.

Waigong stood in front of the picture. I stood behind him. I could not see his face. I only saw his long body, shivering like an old tree when a strong wind passed by. I heard him mumble: *Si le hao, si le hao; si jiushi liao, laio jiushi hao* [Death is good, death is good; death is the end, the end is good].

As Waigong said this to my mother's photo, a hard rain poured down. Thunder and lightning. Every single event about my mother's death was accompanied by a hard rain. I thought of an old Chinese myth about how heaven cries for the unjustly taken lives of the young.

The memorial meeting went almost as smoothly as the city officials expected. The last rite of these memorials was for the officials to shake hands with the family. The solemn hospital official extended his hand toward my father, and my father pushed the hand away. "Just a second," my father said. "What if the person memorialized here is not dead?" Father's question completely surprised everyone. The official's face changed color.

I stepped forward to join my father's questioning. "If my mother were still alive, we would see her in person," I said, "but if my mother is dead, as you claim, we want to see the body. You Party leaders think about it. This is our only demand." Taking a careful look at every one of the officials, I took Waigong's hand and followed my father and brother from the meeting. As we walked out, the sky suddenly cleared.

One of the Party officials hurried after us, promising that they would find Mother's body and have another memorial meeting. My father responded with a cold laugh. We have our small revenge. Through three days of hard rain, the Party officials searched the area in and around the Lotus Flower village. They never found my mother's body. They never will.

FAMILIAR
WEAPONS

Lang Jia is the general manager of an audio and video company in Sichuan. He had just turned forty the day before our interview. He has almost everything that his counterparts in China dream of: a pretty wife, a house of his own, money, and his own car—a Santana (the product of a Volkswagen/Chinese joint venture company) with a car phone.

He looks a bit like the gentry portrayed in classical Chinese novels. He is five feet, five inches tall and a little chubby, and his skin is white and shiny—two signs of being well-off in China. He was born in Lhasa, Tibet's capital city, and his clear, bright eyes reminded me of Tibet's clear, bright skies.

The day of the interview, he was wearing a suede-silk, off-white, short-sleeved shirt; baggy, matte-black, rayon dress trousers; and a pair of hand-made, black leather shoes. The air-conditioning in his Santana was off—he preferred to either roll down the window or use a dramatic black silk fan that was twice the size of a normal fan.

When he returned my call to set up our interview, he called from his car phone and insisted that we meet at the Ling Jiang, a four-star hotel in Chongqing. I was not surprised by his material life. However, sitting in the hotel bar, I was constantly amazed at the juxtaposition of his present life with his earlier experiences.

"Do you know what my name means?" he asked.

"No," I replied. "But it doesn't sound Chinese."

"It's not. It's Tibetan." His words floated in the marbled smoke from his cigarette. "My name was given to me by a monk in Tibet."

When my older brother was born, my father took him to a monk he knew in Tibet and had the monk give my brother his name. The monk named him Ze Ren Lang Jia. Before I was born, my father asked the monk what to name me. The monk told him that I should be given half of my brother's name so that we would grow up together smoothly. My father took Lang Jia from my brother, who then became just Ze Ren. In Tibetan, Ze Ren means "good and honest." Lang Jia means "kind and brave" or "courageous." Now I am not a bad person, but I am not a kind person either. As for brave, well, I did some brave things during the Cultural Revolution, but what I did to my father ...

My father was promoted to the rank of colonel in the KMT army when he was in his early thirties. He rebelled against the KMT and defected to the Chinese Communist Party when Chengdu, the capital of Sichuan Province in southwest China, was peacefully taken by the People's Liberation Army in 1950.

Being a professional soldier was my father's dream as a boy, and he was in his glory in the KMT army. He thought that he would retain his rank after he crossed over to the PLA. Much to his surprise, he was kicked out of the army and sent to a province in southwest China to spend the rest of his life as a clerk. The Party said his transfer was part of the "socialist reconstruction" of the country. While he claimed to believe what they said, I think that deep in his heart he suspected the CCP of removing him from the army because they were afraid that he might promote an uprising of the KMT.

Since he was once a man leading troops, my father was so used to his authority that he was hardly able to adjust himself to his subordinate position in the Commerce Department. At home he would not tolerate my brother and me challenging his authority. In my memory, my father was utterly unreasonable with my brother and me. He preferred to spoil the rod rather than his children. I always thought my father was stone-hearted—that is, until things happened between us during the Cultural Revolution.

The slogan "There Is No Wrong in Revolution; It Is Right to Rebel" swept the country in the autumn of 1967. Many young people were so caught up in revolutionary fever that they joined any kind of gang or faction that declared itself revolutionary. In the early days of the Cultural Revolution, the various factions only engaged in verbal struggles with each other. They were fond of debating who were the true revolutionaries and who were the false—arguing who really stood for the ideals of Chairman Mao. Soon, however, when the verbal struggle could not be won, they resorted to violence. Many cities became ideological and physical battlefields in this struggle. My hometown was a notorious example.

In Chengdu there were two powerful Red Guard factions. One was called Hong Wei Bin Chengdu Budui [The Chengdu Red Guard Unit], also known as Hong Cheng. The other faction was called Ba Er Liu Zaofan Bintuan [August 26th Rebel Unit]. Like most of the youths of that time, I was excited by the Revolution, although I was only thirteen and had no idea what the so-called Revolution was really about. For me, it was a chance to revolt against my father's authority. How could I be wrong? Even Mao approved of rebellion. Remember the popular quotation from Mao? "It is right to rebel." I left home and joined the Hong Cheng.

Headquarters for the Hong Cheng had been established at the University of Telecommunication Engineering in the suburbs of east Chengdu. I moved into the headquarters with the university students who were also members of the group. Close to the university there was a company of the state militia, known as Zhizuo Budui [Supporting Troops of the Left]. The city was getting violent, and the leaders of Hong Cheng wanted weapons. They decided that we would attack the army camp to get some.

The attack took place on a hot and humid afternoon in the autumn of 1967. I had shaved my head and was only wearing boxer shorts. I was to lead eight teenagers, all wearing hand-me-down military uniforms, into a building in the camp.

We found that the staircase to each floor of the building had been blocked with thick wood boards. I saw some university students, who had entered the building basement ahead of us, smashing the barricades with axes, while others climbed into the building through the windows.

We sat back to watch and wait. Soon the barricades were cut through. In one breath I ran up to the third floor, where I encountered a boy running downstairs. He was carrying two guns—a submachine gun on his right shoulder and a pistol in his belt. He looked younger and smaller than I was. Without any hesitation I knocked him to the ground and grabbed the pistol. I thought, Why should a little boy have two guns while I had none?

I left him crying behind me and ran up to the fourth floor with the pistol in my right hand. We had been told that the Zhizuo Budui had hidden their weapons in ceilings because they had heard about our proposed raid. On the fourth floor I kicked a door open. There was nobody there. There was a ladder leaning against the wall. I climbed the ladder to check the ceiling. That cache had already been emptied.

I rushed into the next room. I saw a soldier holding a machine gun standing in the center of the room. I automatically pointed my pistol at his head and shouted, "Freeze!" It was in this moment that I realized the pistol was probably empty—the soldier could shoot me. I tried not to let my fear betray me. After all, the soldier did not know my pistol was empty. We stared at each other for a few seconds. When he showed no sign of wanting to kill me, I tried to take his machine gun. He had a tight grip on the weapon. I kicked him, but he wouldn't let go. I tried to frighten him by threatening him with my pistol. He just grasped his gun more firmly. I realized that he was not afraid of anyone. I changed my tactics and dropped to my knees in front of him suddenly and begged; "Uncle, please give me your gun. I need it to guard Chairman Mao."

He handed me the weapon. I later realized that he wanted me to have the gun. The army was happy to arm the Rebels as long as they thought we were on the same side. It was just a matter of the army saving face by making us look like we had raided the camp for the guns.

Once I took the machine gun, I noticed that it was empty. I asked the soldier for his ammunition, and he said that there were a few boxes of bullets down on the second floor. Carrying the weapon over my shoulder, I went downstairs. He hadn't lied to me. I picked up the largest box, which said it held 300 rounds.

As I came out of the room with the ammunition, a university student who was rushing upstairs grabbed for the box. He was tall and looked strong. I was afraid that there was no way for me to beat him in a fight for the ammunition, and I thought we were both from the Hong Cheng, so I let him have the box without a struggle.

I felt triumphant having captured two guns. No words could describe my pride. That was my day. When we got back to the dormitory, the leaders of Hong Cheng ordered everyone to bring in all the weapons seized from the Zhizuo Budui. The leaders promised redistribution of the weapons after they took inventory. I handed over the machine gun since it had been seen by many people, but I hid the pistol.

Three days later the leaders, all university students, called us together for an oath-taking rally. Everyone was to swear to give his life in defense of Chairman Mao before he was given a weapon. The leader of the rally, who was also in charge of issuing the weapons, was skinny and short, with a dark complexion and short-cropped hair. He gave me one machine gun and five bullets. He made a speech, saying, "We have only half as many guns as there are people, so it is impossible for everyone to have a weapon. Therefore, two of you will share each weapon. We are also short on ammunition, so there will be only five bullets for each weapon. Each bullet has to penetrate an enemy's chest. We pledge to place our young lives in the service of Chairman Mao and to willingly die for his ideals."

After the rally I asked my comrade-in-arms who shared the weapon with me to keep the machine gun, and I kept the bullets. I did not tell him that I had a pistol. That night I went back home with four friends of mine. I felt like I was number one in this world. Nobody dared to look down upon me—I had a pistol with five real bullets.

We lived in a compound of houses surrounding a courtyard, inherited from my paternal grandfather before the 1949 Revolution. I had my own house. This was my first trip home since I left to join the Hong

Cheng. My friends and I brought cigarettes and wine with us. We sat in my house, playing cards and smoking. We were stripped to the waist, hollering, laughing, and beating on the table. The whole room was heavy with the smell of wine, smoke, and sweat. We felt free, independent, and powerful. "We are real men," one of my friends shouted.

No sooner had he shouted than my father threw open the door, cursing me, "You are an evil, wicked boy who deserves to be taken outside and beaten within an inch of his life. You get out of my house. I will not have this kind of a son." He turned the table over, spilling cards and wine on the floor. My friends were paralyzed.

"You get out of here instantly, or prepare to die!" I pulled out my pistol and pointed at my father's head. He stepped back quietly in surprise.

"Listen carefully!" I continued, "Chairman Mao has already urged us to rebel. How dare you try to restrain and discipline me? You are right. I am not your son anymore. I belong to Chairman Mao and to the Revolution."

My father kept stepping back toward the door while I was speaking. I noticed that his eyes were full of surprise and wonder but not fear. I knew he did not fear the pistol; weapons were too long a part of his life. He said nothing and walked out of the house. My friends and I spent the rest of that night drinking and shouting. In the morning we rejoined the Hong Cheng.

I kept making revolution—rebelling against anything anyone labeled counterrevolutionary and doing what I thought was guarding Chairman Mao. I never stopped to think about why my father no longer bothered to talk to me. I took his silence to mean that he did not care about me anymore. Then one day in June of 1971, I realized that my father's love for his children was real, true, forever, and without any conditions.

The central government had just issued new documents discussing the place of educated urban youths in the new society. The instruments urged the Shangshan-Xiaxiang of the educated youths at the age of seventeen. Xiaxiang had two orientations. The first was working with the peasants in rural areas within Sichuan Province. The other was going to

Yunnan Province to work with the Production and Construction Corps along the borders between China, Burma, Laos, and Vietnam. Going to the Construction Corps of Yunnan was called Zhebia. We all were urged to go into the Corps of Yunnan.[1]

The students at the university held many serious discussions about the advantages of Zhebia versus going to the Sichuan countryside. Some said they preferred the corps of Yunnan to the countryside because you got paid by the month and there was a public canteen serving three meals a day. The life in the corps sounded much more exotic and romantic.

And others said they would rather go into the local countryside if they had to leave the city. If you went to the local countryside, you could have one family visit every other year. Additionally, there was still the possibility of returning to the city if you were chosen to be a factory worker or allowed to enlist in the army.

The chances of the youth in the corps returning to Chengdu were close to zero. You might spend the rest of your life out in Yunnan.

I thought that, compared to the local countryside, Zhebia was much better because the corps was under military control. The educated youths working for the corps were paid monthly and issued military uniforms and weapons. Those uniforms and weapons were the biggest attraction to me. I decided to go to Yunnan without thinking twice.

Those of us bound for Yunnan were given a mobilization speech by the local Party leadership. I remember one middle-aged official who stressed the significance of establishing the Production and Construction Corps in Yunnan. The goals of the program were *Daji Di Xiu Fan* [Puncture the Arrogance of Imperialism, Revisionism and the Reactionaries]. The official said that our mission was to help the corps develop rubber tree farms and rubber factories along the border areas. This would strengthen the national defense industry because Western

---

1. Shangshan-Xiaxiang means "Go to the countryside and mountain areas," and Zhebia means "aid for remote areas"—both refer to the practice of sending educated youths to work in the countryside and mountain areas.

capitalists demanded outrageously high prices for their rubber exports to our country. He ended his speech by saying that Zhebia was a patriotic duty and that by going, we were showing our loyalty to the Party.

Accompanying the mobilization speech was an exhibition of sample rubber goods from the plantations and factories. We were totally obsessed by the propaganda. One boy cut his finger with a penknife and wrote a letter with his blood expressing his determination and loyalty.

We would be the first group of Zhebia youths to leave Chengdu. The whole city was stirred up. Fathers and mothers followed their sons and daughters to the railway station, where there was a special train that would carry us to Yunnan.

The rain had been pouring down since early that morning. We scrambled into a truck to head for the railway station. A red paper flower was tied to the front of the truck. It was supposed to symbolize the glory of our generation, but the rain had washed out the color, screwing up the atmosphere a bit. The truck stopped at the People's Square in the southern part of the city. In the center of the square is a statue of Chairman Mao. The statue shows him wearing an overcoat. He has his right arm stretched out and his left arm behind his waist. The statue was a reflection of the then-popular slogan *Mao Zhuxi Huishou Wo Qianjin* [When Chairman Mao Waves His Hand, I Move Forward].

When we arrived at the square, we jumped off the truck and lined up in front of Mao's statue. We raised our right hands and made a solemn vow to Mao. Drops of rain mixed with the tears on our faces and the faces of our parents. After the ceremony, the truck carrying us paraded through the main streets of the city on our way to the railway station, while we cheered and waved our hats.

Unlike my schoolmates, I climbed onto the train alone. No one came to see me off. My mother was in Mao Zedong Sixiang Xuexiban [Study Class of Mao Zedong Thought], and she was not granted permission to leave. My father had been sent to a Gan Xiao in Xichang, the capital of the Liangshan Autonomous Prefecture of the Yi Nationality. He was not allowed to come home to see me off. A few days before I was to leave for Yunnan, my father sent word to me through a friend that he had tried to get leave from the Gan Xiao to see me off but that his request had been rejected. He said that the train would pass by the Gan Xiao, and it might also stop. He would wait for the train by the railway in hopes that he might see me. This was the first time my father showed any concern about me since I pointed my pistol at his head. It was also the first time I knew of his love for me. My younger brother was at the railway station, but he was part of the band that was organized for our send-off and could not get away to say good-bye. As I climbed aboard the train I suddenly felt empty and lonely. I thought of my father and I missed him, even his fists.

The train crept across the countryside for two days and a night, as slow as a snail, making many stops before coming to the Xichang area where the Gan Xiao was situated. I did not know where my father might be waiting for me. Once I heard Xichang announced on the speaker on the train, I kept my forehead pressed to the window of the coach.

The train seemed to speed up as it entered the Xichang area. Suddenly the train made a turn and passed an earth slope in the dusk of the evening. I saw my father holding dried steamed buns and a canteen, standing against the wind on the slope. Although the train seemed to have stopped at every station between Chengdu and Kunming (the capital of Yunnan Province), it didn't stop at that station. I opened the window and leaned out, screaming, "Father! Father!" but the sound of the train swallowed my voice. I felt like my heart was smashed to pieces.

My father must have seen me anyway because I saw him running after the train. He ran clumsily alongside the train, looking for me. I knew that the train might not stop long at Xichang, so I had planned to give him a note. When the train rolled through the station, I thought to throw the paper to my father, but the paper was too light to carry itself away from the train. I had to find something to add weight to the paper, but the only thing I had was a badge of Mao pinned on the right pocket of my shirt. I took it off and wrapped it in the paper. I tossed it from the window and waved one last time. The badge and its message landed far enough away from the train, and I saw my father pick it up. I had written, "Dad, I am leaving. Don't be sad for me. Please forgive me for my disobedience to you in the past."

Many years later my father told me that he and some other parents had waited for that train all day, from dawn till dusk. He thought that going to Zhebia was like going into exile and that he would never see me again.

He never told me if he forgave me or not. But he constantly expressed his regret that he had not been a good father. He said that he had been too tough on me, treating me more like a subordinate in the military than like a son. I was never quite sure what he really meant. But I do not forgive myself for what I did to him that day in his house.

POEMS AND PIGS

Yunsha's name is an unusual one in China. It means "fir tree." Her poet father gave this name to her because the forest was his spirit and the fir tree is symbolic of a strong, straight life force. She is the kind of woman who attracts the attention of men without trying. Although she works hard to avoid such attention, her actions are mostly in vain.

If there is anything special about her appearance, it is her large, hazel eyes. Her friends tease her about having Western blood. Because she is in her mid-thirties, her friends push her to marry. She says that she will always look for love but never marry. For her, marriage does not mean "family." It is just a legal definition. "Family is part of a value system," she says, "and the law doesn't set values."

Yun Sha is not chic, but she is clothes and color smart. She is good at putting different outfits together by exploiting her interest and taste in folk art. When we met in a teahouse in Guangzhou in the summer of 1991, she was wearing a peasant skirt in black with a gold, Indian folklore motif. Above that she wore a Mexican, high-waisted, white, sleeveless blouse embroidered with small white flowers. For jewelry, she wore a bronze leopard necklace from Tibet and a silver lotus bracelet from the Qing dynasty.[1]

Yunsha is pretty, pleasant, and cheerful. Only when she looks into your eyes and begins to speak her thoughts do you realize that there is an extreme sadness in her heart. Like many who bear the sadness of the Cultural Revolution, her emotions are contagious.

---

1. The lotus is a symbol of purity in China.

I was an extremely sensitive child. The doctor said this was because my father and mother were going through their first political struggles while I was still swimming in my mother's womb. That was 1958, when the whole country was caught up in the Antirightist Campaign. My father was a well-known poet, and my mother was famous for her sharp, analytical newspaper stories. Like many young intellectuals, my parents firmly believed in the Party and took what Mao had to say in his Hundred Flowers speech to heart. They thought they were the vanguard of society.

At Mao's bidding my father began to write about Chinese society and how it could change. Ultimately, like all of the naive people who believed Mao's lies, my parents suffered for their faith. They were still under suspicion when I was born in mid-1958. My mother often says that the reason I am so sensitive to what other people are thinking and feeling is because she was pregnant with me during those long, dark days. As she carried me she worried each day whether or not my father would be branded a rightist and if he would return from work. They survived the Antirightist Campaign, but before they could lean back and take a deep breath, another witch-hunt found them in the summer of 1966.

I was my father's favorite, his only daughter. He loved to spoil me, and I frequently took advantage of the situation. I remember once I accompanied him to the barbershop. I was the only child there, and as I was waiting for him, I complained loudly about how bored I was.

"Oh, you're bored?" my father said. "Let's do something interesting. How about a haircut?"

I didn't really know what he meant, but I said, "Sure!"

The barber asked me how I wanted my hair to look, and I pointed at my father's head. Quite quickly my long hair was on the floor, and I was waltzing out the door hand in hand with my father. My father was amused, and I felt free from all that hair.

On the way home from the barber's, he bought me a helium balloon. We walked down the street with the balloon floating over my head. I had never seen a balloon like this before, and I thought if I let it go, it would float down into my hand. It didn't.

"Where is it going?" I asked my father as the balloon floated away. "When will it come back?"

He was amused and said, "No, it will not come back to this city. It's going to some faraway land."

I began to cry. However, at that moment a cotton-candy vendor passed us by. Intrigued, I lost interest in my disappearing balloon.

"What's that stuff, Father?" I asked.

"You know what it is," he replied.

"No, I don't," I said, testing his willingness to indulge me.

"Really? Well, it's a kind of candy," my father said, giving me a knowing look, adding, "I guess you don't know how candy tastes either. Right?" Before I said anything, he called the vendor and bought me some cotton candy.

When we arrived home, my mother was not especially pleased, however. "What happened to your hair?" she asked me.

"I was bored," I replied.

"What's the matter with you?" she asked my father. "Were you bored, too? Or are you trying to turn your daughter into a boy?"

I could always count on my father to bail me out of the trouble I seemed to find. On another occasion I left the house to go swimming with some of my friends. In those days there were two places to swim in my hometown: a public pool surrounded by bleachers and stalls for changing your clothes and a more private pool with showers and locker rooms. My mother had given me the money to go to the private pool, but my three friends wanted to save their money for popsicles. I was afraid that if I would not go with them, they might not play with me anymore.

At the pool we changed into our suits and left our clothes in the bleachers at the side of the pool. An hour later when we were done swimming, we went to get our clothes and mine were missing. My brand-new pink dress, brand-new sandals, and underwear had been stolen. I didn't know what to do. I could not walk home wearing just a wet bathing suit, so I asked my friends to go to my house and tell my parents what happened. I waited by the side of the pool for about an hour until one of the women who worked there came up to me and said; "It's time for us to close. Come with me and I will get you some clothes from the lost and found. You can bring them back later."

I dressed myself in some boys' baggy shorts and a T-shirt and started walking home. I was almost at the exit of the swimming pool park when my father came riding up on his dark green, German-made bicycle.

"Oh, my little imp," he said as he stopped in front of me, "whose clothes are you wearing?"

"I don't know. Some boy's, I guess," I said, looking at his shoes.

"Do you want another swim?" Dad asked. I thought he was being sarcastic.

"But we don't have any tickets," I answered.

"Oh, yes we do," he answered, pulling a pair of tickets to the private pool from his shirt pocket.

Forgetting how guilty I had felt only moments before, I climbed onto his handlebars and off we went.

When we arrived home, two hours late for dinner, my mother was extremely angry. She said, "The little devil went to the wrong pool and lost her clothes. The big devil was sent to rescue her and got lost himself!"

My father smiled and replied, "Shall we have dinner now since the little devil and the big devil are all home safely?"

You shouldn't get the idea that my father was a poor parent. Quite the contrary. He was a scholar of the Chinese classics and could read the works of the old scholars in the original.[2] He encouraged me to study hard and to live according to Confucian morality. He often took me to the teahouses where he met with his literary colleagues and included me in the discussions from an early age. It was his intention that I should become a scholar in the classic sense and not just a college-educated parrot like so many young people of that, and this, day.

---

2. This is a little like being able to read Chaucer in the original. Ancient Chinese has no punctuation and is open to interpretation and misinterpretation, making it difficult to read and understand.

My parents' troubles began again in the summer of 1966. School was out and I was home reading. I especially liked the newspaper, even though I did not understand everything they printed. My favorite part of the paper was the cultural section, where they published my father's poetry. Usually his poetry appeared on the front page under his name, printed in big characters. This day's article was different. I didn't understand the characters in the title. Relying on a pocket Chinese dictionary, I read through the title: "Down with the Bourgeois Poet Fu Shan." I did not quite understand what bourgeois meant, but I knew "Down with" was bad.

My dad was in his study writing. He usually started his work each morning about nine o'clock and worked until late in the evening, breaking for lunch and dinner. I did not want him to read that newspaper, so I buried it in my grandmother's knitting basket. My mother came home for lunch early that day. This was strange because she was always late.

More strange was that Mom did not ask me about my study. That was the first thing she would check when she came home for lunch. That day she walked in and asked me where Dad was. She did not really expect an answer, however; she knocked at the door of Dad's study.

"Mom, what does bourgeois mean?" I stopped her.

"Where did you hear that word?" she responded.

"From the newspaper," I said, adding, "They said down with Dad, too."

"From now on you are not supposed to read the newspapers anymore," Mom ordered, disappearing into Dad's study. Her voice was so firm that I did not dare even to ask her why.

I could hear Mom and Dad whispering in his study. They did not come out for lunch until Grandma had reheated the food twice. I liked lunchtime. Dad always had something interesting and humorous to say at the table. He was absolutely silent that day. I noticed that he did not even touch the dish of fried eggs with tomatoes, his favorite. Mom kept pushing him to eat, saying, "Everything will be all right." His only response was a deep sigh.

Nothing happened that afternoon. "It will be all right," Mom told Dad again in the evening when they were retiring to their bedroom.

It was about midnight when I was awakened by a loud knocking at the door. "Who is it?" Grandma turned on the light in the living room.

"Open the door," those outside ordered, beating harder on the door. "This is a check on the household occupants."

Grandma was about to open the door, but Mom stopped her. Mom said, "It's nothing serious. Go back to sleep." Then Mom walked into my bedroom and said, "Stay here. Don't move and don't look—no matter what happens." She closed my door.

I waited until she left, and then I opened the door and peeked out through the crack. No sooner had Mom opened the door than a group of young men rushed in. They were wearing army helmets and green uniforms and holding iron bars. One of them pushed my mother against the wall, while others shouted, "Where is the reactionary poet? Hand him over."

Before Mom could say anything, one of them kicked in the door to my father's study. Two others dragged my mother into my parents' bedroom, just across the hall from mine. There was a glass-front book case in the bedroom where Dad kept his rare, out-of-print books and his own publications. One man smashed the front of the case with his iron bar. The shattered glass rained down on the floor. Dad stood absolutely still in the middle of the room. One of the other Rebels swept all the books out onto the floor. They dug out the copies of Dad's books, ignoring the others. One of them waved a book and barked, "All your writing is counterrevolutionary, contrary to the ideals of Chairman Mao and the socialist state. It is all *du sao* [poisonous weeds]. It will be destroyed!" Two of the Rebels forced Dad to his knees. The leader tried to make Dad admit that his writings were harmful. When Dad refused to do so, he was slapped.

The Rebels put all of the books into gunnysacks. They ordered Dad to write a confession and deliver it to the Red Flag Troop the next day.[3] Dad pleaded with the Rebels not to destroy the other books, saying,

"You can criticize me as much as you want, but please do not destroy the other books. Some of them are precious and rare."

They only laughed at him as they dragged the gunnysacks out of the house.

All of a sudden everything was quiet again. I went to Mom and Dad's bedroom and asked; "Are they all bad guys?"

"No," Dad said, "they are just too young to understand a lot of things. Go back to sleep. Remember I am going to test you tomorrow on the three hundred Tang poems. How many can you recite now?"

The next day when I got up, Mom was not there. Neither was Dad. Mom came home late that day. Dad did not. Grandma asked Mom to go out looking for Dad. She sounded like he was lost somewhere, like a child. Mom said Dad was at a meeting and wouldn't come back til after midnight.

Dad didn't come home that night or the next day either. Two days later a Rebel came to our house. He told Mom to send some clothes to Dad, who was being held in a Study Class for Mao Zedong Thought.

Dad was held in the study class for two months. The day he was released he was sent to a remote area for reform through labor. Soon thereafter Mom was sent to a reform through labor farm in a mountain area to work alongside those who had committed real crimes. She was accused of writing stories that cherished capitalism.

I was left with Grandma. Each night when I went to bed, she told me that when I opened eyes the next morning, Mom and Dad would be standing by my bed. Each morning I would ask Grandma where they were. She would say that their train was delayed. She knew and I knew it was just a hopeless dream, but I never tired of hearing it.

My friend Li Sha lived alone upstairs. Her father had been killed in a local jail where he had been held as a rightist at the beginning of the

---

3. The Red Flag Troop was the most notorious revolutionary Rebel organization in the province.

Cultural Revolution. Her mother was sent to the same farm as my Dad because she had tried to clear the accusations against her husband.

After Mom and Dad were sent away, I had looked for Dad's publications. They had all been carried off by the Rebels in that sudden midnight raid. The only thing I could find was a copy of "Night Scene." I read it to Li Sha. She loved it so much that she hand-copied it in her notebook.

We frequently talked about visiting her mom and my dad, but we were too poor to afford the long-distance bus fare. Both of us lived on a small amount of money. Our parents' salaries had been deeply cut when they were sent to jail. The Party said traitors and their children did not deserve a decent life.

One summer evening Li Sha came to my house. She said she had a friend who drove a truck for the military and was willing to take us to the labor reform farm. The only condition was that we had to leave early the next morning and come back the same day. I agreed.

I had not seen Dad for a year and a half. I knew I had to bring something delicious for him. He loved cookies, but the whole country was busy making revolution instead of making decent food. It didn't make any difference. I didn't have any money to buy cookies even if they were available. The only thing I did have was a hen that I kept as a pet. Grandma had given her to me when my parents disappeared. I called the hen Little Whiskers because she had some black feathers under her beak that looked like whiskers.

When she heard my plan to make soup of my pet, Grandma asked me, "Are you sure?"

I said, "Yes." Then I let Little Whiskers out of her pen. Some people say that animals can understand human plans and feelings, and I believe it. Little Whiskers refused to come out when I opened the door. As soon as Grandma tried to grab her and drag her out, she flew out of the cage and around the courtyard. The whole compound could hear Grandma calling the hen and chasing her around the courtyard. "Little Whiskers, you come home. I won't kill you," Grandma said.

Soon she was out of breath, so I had to get the hen by myself. I mimicked Little Whiskers' clucking and put some rice on the ground while walking backward into the house. Little Whiskers followed the trail of rice right into the house, where I grabbed her and handed her to Grandma, who killed her and boiled her.

About five o'clock the next morning, Li Sha and I climbed into the military truck. While the truck was going through the city, the ride wasn't too bad. But when we got outside of town on the rural roads, the dust whirled behind the truck, and Li Sha and I were tossed around like popcorn.

I was carrying my soup of Little Whiskers in a small, covered clay-ware cooking dish. Every time the truck would hit a bump, the soup would splash and spill out of the top. I tried to keep the soup inside by holding the pot in my hands instead of resting it on the floor of the truck or on my knees. I held my arms in the same position for five hours, but no matter how hard I had tried to keep the chicken soup from spilling, by the time we reached the farm, there was only dry chicken meat left in the pot.

By ten o'clock that morning our truck was rocking down a muddy, narrow country road. Although it was harvest time, I did not see any peasants working the rice fields. Later I learned that the harvest and postharvest production were the work of the denounced intellectuals like my Dad.

The labor reform farm was a group of small, gray buildings, as common as any residential complex in a small town. The only differences were a high fence and an armed soldier standing at the entrance.

Li Sha's friendly driver dropped the two of us by the side of a rice field, about one hundred meters from the entrance. Li Sha, who was five years older than I was, walked in front as we headed for the gate. She said if the soldier was going to shoot us, she would cover me up.

The gate guard didn't see us until we were about twenty meters from the gate. "Stop there," he shouted. But we did not stop moving toward.

"If you move one more step, I'll fire." I could hear him loading his gun.

We continued toward the gate.

The soldier raised his gun and aimed at us.

"He's really going to shoot, " Li Sha's voice was shaking. "But I have to see my mom."

"Me, too," I said. Maybe I was too young to understand danger, but the soldier did not match my image of a bad guy. In his twenties, he seemed like a farm boy, perhaps a bit taller than the average of his rural brothers.

"Uncle Soldier, please let us in," I asked. "My dad is inside." I didn't look at his face but at his gun. I was afraid that he might pull the trigger.

He did not shoot but pushed me away with his gun. Then he pushed Li Sha so hard that she fell down. Li Sha countered by reciting Mao's quotation "We'll not attack unless we are attacked; if we are attacked, we will certainly counterattack." Then she blinked at me, suggesting that I steal into the compound.

I sneaked past the guard as he argued with Li Sha about Chairman Mao. While I was wondering which building I should go into, a tall man appeared carrying two steaming wooden buckets. The man was walking toward me. He was tall and bony, and the load on his right shoulder was so heavy it bowed his back. His trousers were rolled up to reveal his too-skinny legs. His profile reminded me of movie portrayals of peasants enslaved by the exploiting class.

The tall man stopped. He breathed on his glasses and cleaned them with his handkerchief, checking them in the air. The way he examined his glasses was so familiar that I knew he had a mole at the outside corner of his right eye.

"Daddy," I burst out.

Dad was clearly astounded. He paused a second to make sure what he heard was real. "Dad," I called again. He turned around, taking off his glasses and putting them back on. We looked at each other. I could feel the light of sadness, sorrow, and love in his eyes, touching my hair, my cheeks, my heart.

"I have to go feed the pigs now before their food gets cold," he said, bending over to shoulder the two buckets of pig feed.

"Pigs?" I couldn't believe my ears. "What about your poetry?"

My naive question was heartbreaking for Dad.

"No poetry now, just pigs," Dad said quietly. "I am a swineherd."

"But you can still test me on the three hundred Tang poems, right?"

"I am afraid not." Dad turned and walked toward the pigsty. I followed him. After he fed the pigs, he took off his glasses again and rubbed his eyes. I saw tears in his eye. But he wiped them away.

"I can remember your 'Night Scene' now."

What a shame. I could now remember this poem. Every time Dad or Mom asked me to read it before, I always refused to do so. Dad always excused me by saying, "My little imp is just too modest for me."

Now I thought to recite Dad's poem was the best way to comfort him.

> *Tightly in its arms,*
> *The forest is holding the moon;*
> *Twinkling through coniferous trees,*
> *Are the green lights of the moon and stars.*

"Please stop." Dad covered my mouth with his hand. "Dear daughter, Daddy knows you can. But don't," he insisted firmly. "The Party says my poems are poisonous weeds."

Dad turned back to his work, pouring the feed into the pig trough, the ribs in his back showing through his thin shirt. The father and poet I knew was gone.

Suddenly Dad said, "Leave now. Quickly." Before I understood what he was talking about, two men were standing on the other side of the pigsty. One was a soldier carrying a rifle with a fixed bayonet. The other was a man I knew as Uncle Zhou. He used to come visiting Dad and Mom with his wife. He had been the head of the provincial library. I called to him, "Hello, Uncle Zhou." He stared at me as if he had never seen me before. Then he told my father, "They sent me for you. Be careful." Dad lifted the bucket from the pig trough and stretched his back. His sad eyes fixed on my face as if to say good-bye; then he turned and walked away, followed by Uncle Zhou. I watched him shuffle away. Dad turned one more time to wave to me. I tried to wave to him and realized that I was still holding the chicken soup.

"Dad, chicken soup," I said, running after him. The soldier pointed his bayonet at me. I was scared and did not move anymore. I begged the soldier to give the chicken soup to Dad. He took the soup from me without saying anything. I stood there watching the soldier escort Dad and Uncle Zhou into cell building number 103.

I never figured out whether Dad tasted my chicken soup or not. A few years later, when the Cultural Revolution was over and Dad was allowed to come home, I did not dare ask him about that visit. I was afraid that reminders would drag Dad into that age of darkness again.

Many years later I went back to the labor reform farm. The farm had been replaced by a factory. Pointing to a marble building, I told a local official, "There used to be a Party concentration camp here. Right there was cell number 103. In that cell a true communist poet died."

The local official, much younger than me, said I was crazy and misled. "Once upon a time, this was a huge manor," he said. "Many poor peasants died here because of the landlord's cruel exploitation."

A TREAT FOR
MY FATHER

Xiaohong is the only one of three sisters who has not gone to the United States in search of a different life. As a result, she is the one to whom it fell to care for her mother when she came down with Alzheimer's disease. And although Xiaohong is still young, she seems older and more serious than either of her sisters. And serious is the word for her: serious look, serious dress, and a serious attitude toward life and her job. I know from talking to her sisters that she never complains of the problems of living in China.

I interviewed Xiaohong at a publishing house in Beijing where she is a senior editor. Her office is small and filled to the ceiling with boxes of manuscripts, magazines and journals, books, and stationery. She is a bit taller than either of her sisters, five feet, eight inches, with a few gray hairs among the black. She was dressed in a tan skirt and a plain white blouse.

In contrast to what her sister Xiaozhong had told me, it seemed to me that Xiaohong was rational, locking her emotions away from the public and her sisters. She was not so quiet, however, as she recounted her story for me. Her story was accompanied by many tears.

The Cultural Revolution? Well, politics was completely crazy during those years. The CCP refused to trust anyone who had come from landed or middle-class family backgrounds, even longtime Party members from those classes. The Party only trusted illiterate peasants and the working class. And the army. Mao Zedong said, it was necessary for the educated people of the cities to go to the countryside and be reeducated by the peasants.

My father came from a wealthy, landed family in the south part of China. Because of his family background and his status as an intellectual, my father was accused of being a traitor to the Party. He was stripped of his position as the general manager of the government publishing house in Beijing. A traitor? My father? Nothing could have been more ridiculous. In his teenage years my father had rebelled against his rich family and had plunged into the revolutionary movement. During the 1940s, he had helped pool money and goods the Party badly needed. Now he was being repaid.

My sister Xiaozhong was the first of our family to be taken away, sent to the countryside to be "reeducated" by those illiterates. Soon afterward my mother was sent to the Mao Zedong Sixiang Xuexiban.[1] Although this "school" was in Beijing, where we lived, my mother was not allowed to come home. At the age of thirteen I was left to take care of my father and my younger sister, Xiaoming.

I remember the moment my father took my sister Xiaoming and myself into our living room. On the central wall, where a classical Chinese painting had hung, was now a portrait of Chairman Mao. The classical Chinese poems by artists known for their calligraphy that had flanked the painting were also missing, replaced by cheap prints of Mao's quotations in his script. I still remember two of them: "Serve the people heart and soul," and "Fight selfishness. Repudiate revisionism." My father took my younger sister's hand and mine in his. Standing between us in front of the portrait of Mao, he said quietly to Mao's portrait, "Trust the Party. Trust the masses."

Now I frequently think of what my father said that day in front of that picture. He knew what was happening in China, but he didn't have the heart to make our life miserable or difficult by explaining. He probably thought that I was too young to understand him or the politics of the situation. But I knew he needed somebody to talk to. His own spiritual burden needed to be shared. The Party had turned against him,

---

1. This was the Study Class for Mao Zedong Thought.

and once you lost your credit with them, your political and work career came to an end. Your political tragedies could also ruin your children's future. I knew that's why my father was feeling sorry for us.

The Cultural Revolution also turned a lot of people into Judases. My father never reported anyone to the Party. However, as the Cultural Revolution progressed, he was reluctant to trust anyone either. He believed in and trusted the Party and the masses. But neither the Party nor the masses ever returned his trust. In 1967 he was arrested and sent to the Gan Xiao in Hubei Province, central China. He was charged with being a *zouzipai*.[2] Imagine, the intellectual power of such a wonderful old man was put to work raising a few hundred ducks. I normally cannot bear to think about it.

Sometime around the Spring Festival in 1970, my sister Xiaozhong and I were granted permission to visit our father in the countryside.[3] This was the first time we were allowed to see him since he was sent away. Travel for personal reasons was expensive during the Cultural Revolution. Fortunately for us, the government had continued to pay our father a small salary during his reeducation so we had money for railway fare. We traveled first to Shanghai to see my father's older brother. The two brothers were dearly close to each other.

Now Chinese tradition says that when you make a visit to a family member or a friend, you are supposed to bring that person some food as a gift. The best gifts are local delicacies or something that demands skillful preparation on the part of the bearer. We were too young to really understand this, and we had not prepared anything for our father. I was so excited about being able to see him again that I did not think about anything else. I felt so happy. But my uncle said that it was not right to go to him empty-handed. Since Shanghai enjoys a reputation for exceptional desserts, he sent my aunt to buy some biscuits and other desserts for us to take to my father.

---

2. *Zouzipai* is a "capitalist-roader."
3. The Spring Festival is the traditional Chinese New Year.

As we continued on our trip, I carried the desserts in my schoolbag. I remember imagining how much my father would enjoy the desserts and how he would tease me as he always did when he received a gift. The picture came into my mind, clear and vivid, reminding me how much I missed him. I did not want to seem weak, and I did not want my sister to see me crying, so I bent my head over my bag, pretending to check the desserts as the tears came.

I was born and raised in Beijing, where the winters are dry and cold. This was my first time making a trip to the south in the wintertime. The weather at that time of year was damp and cold, typical winter weather for the south of China. There were no heating facilities in the second-class carriage, and we rode on hard wooden seats. I felt like the blood was frozen in my fingers and toes and the blood circulation of my whole body was blocked. The blood in my heart, however, was warm with anticipation. My face was hot and red with excitement.

It took us one day and night to get to Hubei. My father was not in his room when my sister and I arrived. He was out working in the fields. One of his two roommates, an elderly man, volunteered to go find my father. The elderly man told us that he was home sick that day; otherwise he would be working in the fields as well.

After the elderly man left, I had a chance to look around my father's living quarters. There was no kitchen and no bathroom. Although the dwelling was separate from the others, this so-called house had in fact only one small room, in which my father and another two men ate, slept, and wrote the required self-criticism for the authorities of the CCP. In the center of the room was a knee-high table. Under the table were three short bamboo chairs. This, I thought, was the total living space for three old men?

Since the house lacked kitchen facilities, I dug a knife and one of the desserts out my bag. I cut it into bite-sized pieces and put them into an enamel mug I found on the table. On the top of the dessert I placed a note reading, "Father, I beg you eat these secretly!" and then I put the lid on the mug. Whenever my father had something delicious, he always shared it with someone else. Selfishly, I did not want anybody other than my father to taste our gifts.

My father's roommate soon came back from the fields, saying that no one was allowed to leave before lunchtime. We would have to wait until one o'clock before we could see our father. When he finally appeared, I was as stunned as if someone had struck me in the head. He looked like a piece of paper, pale and lightweight, but his skin was darker than any paper. The wind could have blown him away. He was really old looking but with one exception: His hair had not turned gray. It was still black and neat.

When my father walked into the room, he acted as though he did not remember who I was. When I burst out crying, "Dad, it's us, Xiaozhong and Xiaohong," he half opened his mouth, pausing in the air as if he was seeking his power of speech or the memory of his relation to us. It was so miserable to see him in that condition. Where was our humorous and cheerful father, usually so full of wit? First he stuttered a greeting and then hurried from the room to buy lunch in the canteen of the Gan Xiao. When my father came back from the canteen, the other two men removed themselves from the table to their own beds, sitting there to eat.

The "lunch" my father returned with was almost inedible. All he had to eat was coarse rice with some thin soup made from some kind of canned vegetable. My father apologized for the food, saying that there was rarely anything else to eat in the camp. I could hardly imagine that my father had to eat this every day of his life. As I learned later, this kind of treatment was normal in the reeducation camps for *zouzipai*. In the Party's view, people in these places were expected to become so humble that they would eat whatever was served, even food a pig would refuse. My father easily ate up two bowls of this horrible rice. Each bowl held about one-half cup of rice. I wondered how his stomach was capable of accepting such awful food.

My sister and I exchanged glances, and then we looked at our father and at the lunch in front us. Silence overwhelmed the house. Looking at the bowl of soup on the table, I could see my father's clouded face reflected there, floating with a few vegetable leaves. "What? Is this soup or an edible mirror?" I muttered, trying to release my anger and lighten the mood in the room. No one responded, but I could sense my father's eyes inspecting me. I looked up into his face, and I could see that he was laughing at me for being so picky. I dropped my head and stuck my chopsticks into my rice bowl, stirring the soup up and down, up and down, without tasting the food. My chopsticks unexpectedly struck something soft at the bottom of the bowl. It must be sausage, I thought. The smell of sausage rushed into my nose and the taste of sausage into my mouth. I love sausage. I looked back into my father's eyes and saw a light that I was quite familiar with. He loved to give us children gifts. These gifts did not have to be expensive or fancy. Usually they were something like a cute pencil, or a storybook, or candies and cookies. Whenever we were happily surprised, we could see the light of love twinkling in his eyes. I dug up the soft thing from the bottom of my bowl. What caught my eyes was no sausage but a preserved egg. In the meantime my sister found another egg buried at the bottom of her bowl. I was surprised, but with disappointment rather than happiness. "I do not care for preserved egg," I said quietly. I removed the egg and placed it in my father's bowl. I noticed the light of love dim in his eyes, replaced by sorrow and guilt.

I have since come to understand and regret what I said to him that day. I was such an inconsiderate and juvenile girl, without any way of understanding how much my words might hurt my father. I now realize that my words hurt him deeply. But as was his way, he did not say anything about my inconsiderate remark. He just sighed deeply. It was his roommate, sitting on his bed by the wall, who told me not to put any more weight in my father's heart. He told us that my father bought the preserved eggs from the canteen during the Dragon Boat Festival (the fifth day of the fifth lunar month) more than a half-year ago. Each person at the Gan Xiao was allowed to purchase two eggs. The Party said that reforming *zouzipai* was the Party's historical mission. The *zouzipai* were not entitled to decent food. They were accused of having "capitalist" stomachs that needed to be properly "socialized." The two eggs were not simply eggs. They were the expression of the Party's human sympathy. My father had saved the eggs.

"Oh!" my father said. "You never liked preserved eggs? I'm so sorry, but this is the only thing I can provide that would improve the meal." These were the first words he had said to me since our arrival. His voice was full of guilt and carried a message far beyond an apology for the food he was serving us. I was uncertain what it was for a moment. I couldn't help looking into his eyes again, looking for a reason for his sorrow. His eyes reflected a melancholy emotional sea with a calm surface but turbulent bottom. They reminded me of the days before he left home for the Gan Xiao.

Looking at his sad face, I tried to cheer him up. "Father, don't you want to find our secret here? I mean a real secret." I passed him the mug containing the dessert. I was hoping he would read the note and realize that I did not blame him for his problems. I wanted him to know that I loved him and missed him. He lifted the lid of the mug and read the note. His hands began to tremble and his eyes filled. However, he did not cry. He did not say anything to me, and he did not taste the dessert either. He just patted me on the head, letting out another deep sigh. In my ignorance, I did not know how to comfort him. I mean, what I was supposed to do? Hug him? No. That's not the Chinese way. So I sat there quietly.

After lunch I wanted to do something to ease my guilty feelings and to cover my awkwardness at the same time. I wanted to wash his bedding. I knew that such work was too heavy for him in his state of health. My heart began to really ache when I cleared his narrow single bed. There was no mattress or any other soft, warm items like the cotton-padded quilts that are otherwise so ubiquitous in Chinese households. On the bed frame were some unpolished wood boards, and on the boards was a straw pallet, thin and damp. His only covering was a worn blanket. I doubted that it could keep out either the cold or the humidity, especially since my father's bed was by the window.

My father was neat and clean. He had folded the blanket in a square, military style. On the top of the blanket he placed his pillow. The bed was then entirely covered with a piece of plastic. He said he had been unable to wash the bedding since he arrived in this camp a year and a half before, yet it was still reasonably clean.

It was a fifteen-minute walk to the pond where my father did his wash. The water seemed clean and deep. It reminded me of my father, clean, pure, and innocent. Both of them, my father and the pond, deserved better than they were getting in this place.

There was little I could do for my father here, nothing except cleaning his house and washing his clothes. But I could not do even these trivial things for him every day. I would have to leave soon. Life under such circumstances was so difficult. But the Party would not let its prisoners die. Neither could prisoners commit suicide because such action would place their children in jeopardy. Suicide was seen as bringing humiliation upon the Party, which would then retaliate against the living. Suddenly I realized that I was crying, ice-cold tears running down my face, dropping from my chin. I was pinched with cold. *

The Party bureaucrats at the Gan Xiao had imposed a two-day limit on visits by relatives. It was terribly unfair. We had waited three years to see our father but were only allowed to be with him for forty-eight hours. How many hours are there in three years?

Early on the third day before we left for home, my father took my sister and me to a downtown restaurant for lunch. He told us that the restaurant served Wuchang fish but that only two fish were served per day.[4] Therefore, we needed to get there early. However, our father had not been to the restaurant before. There was only one fish left when we got to the restaurant. The other one had been ordered by an elderly man for his daughter. We stopped to talk to them and found out that, like us, his daughter was visiting him at Gan Xiao. But their situation was much better. This man had been found innocent of any political wrongdoing. He was waiting for the Party to call him back to Beijing, where he expected to return to his previous position in the government.

---

4. Wuchang, a city of Hubei Province, is well known for this kind of fish, a blunt-snout bream, so it is named after Wuchang.

After lunch the old man and his daughter planned to climb Lushan Mountain.[5]

At the restaurant I felt like we were having our last meal together. I didn't know if or when I would see my father again. I did not notice how the fish tasted, although it was rare and expensive. My father seemed to feel the same way. He concentrated on cutting as many bones from the fish as possible and serving my sister and me. He did not taste the fish at all. When my sister and I tried to serve him some of the fish, he pushed the dish back at us, saying, "Eat more. Eat more."

After lunch it was time to go to the railway station. The station was a sea of many heads floating up and down and hands stretching out, reaching back and forth. People on the platform were trying to touch hands with their friends and relatives on the train. Those on the train were stretching out of the windows, reaching for those on the platform.

My sister and I managed to get through the crowd and onto the train. We pushed our way through the crowded car with our elbows, trying to reach the windows. Those we pushed aside cursed us. "What's your hurry? Do you have an appointment at the cemetery?"[6] My sister warned me to ignore them. She knew that holding my tongue was not my way. Such treatment was humiliating. But for the sake of my father I did not return the curses. I did not want to worry him, but I wanted desperately to take one last look at him before the train left. A young man was wedged next to a window.

I squeezed forward and asked him, "Comrade, I beg you, let me share half of the window. My father is out there."

Maybe it was the despair in my voice or perhaps because I was a girl. In any case, he gave up his spot without saying anything. I took advantage of a chance to drag my sister up next to me. From the window I could see that my father was jammed in among the crowd. "Father, here

---

5. Lushan Mountain is a popular scenic attraction in China.

6. This humorous Chinese curse implies the other person is already dead and therefore should not hurry since the only place she or he is going is to the next world. There is no reason to hurry to the graveyard; it will be open when the person gets there.

we are!" I screamed as loudly as I could. He was so tall and had such long arms that his hands were able to reach ours as he stood by the train.

At that moment, the arms reaching up and down toward each other seemed to be bridges linking lives across an abyss of death. People felt as though they had to reach someone, whether or not they knew the person whom they were touching. My father's hands touched mine briefly and then suddenly were lost, and mine were firmly grasped by the hands of someone else.

The train whistle sounded. It reminded me of the folk saying "The devil rings his bell when he comes to get your life." The whistle brought everyone in the station to tears. My sister burst out crying. My father was carried away from the window by the crowd. He tried to reach our hands again and again. But he failed. Now the train began to move. My father stood there, looking frightened and hopeless, crying with his mouth half open. This was the only time I ever saw him cry. As the train left the platform I got my last look at my father, shaking and bent over at the waist, moaning.

His face and voice have haunted me ever since. I know I grew up to be a different kind of person than my father expected. My father was a generous and forgiving man. Well, sentimental, too. He would have wanted me to grow up and be generous and forgiving, but I am not. I don't want to forgive or forget. Because of the Cultural Revolution, my father's life was a complete tragedy.

IRON GRANDMA

The newspaper where Zhanmei works is located in a commercial center in Beijing. When I arrived at the main entrance, I found that the street was barred to through traffic of all kinds. The guards there were only allowing bicycles and automobiles to enter if the drivers or riders were employed inside the center. By the time I rode around to the visitor's gate, I was thirty minutes late for my appointment.

Zhanmei showed no impatience at my late arrival—patience is one quality many of our generation acquired during the Cultural Revolution. She was dressed all in black, a rayon blouse over a crewneck shirt, ankle-length black skirt, and a black leather belt. Expensive clothing for a Chinese. The rayon blouse had a few red and yellow flowers embroidered across the bodice, toning down an otherwise severe outfit.

When she talked, her head nodded and her short hair bounced back and forth. Her eyes were large for a Chinese, and her voice was musical but calm. She listened to my questions quietly, and when she talked, she spoke slowly and softly, as though she were telling me someone else's story.

My family was different from most in China in the 1960s. I was raised in a *nu ren guo* [an empire of women]. By the time the Cultural Revolution began, my father and my grandfather had both been dead for a long time. Our family consisted of my *wai zu* [maternal grandmother], my *da yi* [mother's older sister], my mother and five children: four girls and one boy, my younger brother.

I was extremely close to our *wai zu* when I was little. I was her pet. She was in her eighties, graceful and elegant. Her waist was straight, her hair shiny, her mind clear and sharp. She read the *People's Daily* every day. In classical terms she was still a *sipin furen*.[1]

I remembered she never called Mao Chairman Mao. Instead, she called him by his full name Mao Zedong. Mao was such a god at that time. The whole country called him our beloved Chairman Mao. Whenever I heard her saying, Mao Zedong, I would correct her. "Wai Zu, how can you call him by name? You shouldn't. You should call him Chairman Mao." She always gave a curious smile in response.

One day as I was about to correct her again, she stopped me by saying, "Everyone has a name. His is Mao Zedong. His is like yours, given to identify him. Why should I not call him by name? I am older than he is. Why should I call him by his position?" There was no way to argue with her. She was a great woman. She had experienced the chaos of two wars and the changes from the feudalism of the Qing dynasty through to the "socialism" of the CCP. She was afraid of nothing.

I was a teenager in a high school in Beijing in 1966 when the Cultural Revolution began. I now wish I had been much older. Maybe then I would not have been so timid and would not have hurt my family the way I did.

In Beijing autumn is the best season of the year. The weather is warm without being hot or sticky; the sky is usually clear. One afternoon the sunshine sky filled with black clouds. They did not seem to promise rain, however. They looked odd. They reminded me of a story told by my *wai zu*. She told me that the last emperor was brought down from his throne on a day when bizarre clouds floated in the sky. I almost always believed what Wai Zu told me, even though sometimes her sayings sounded superstitious.

On this day what my *wai zu* said about odd clouds came true. The Red Guards in my class forced me to go with them to search a classmate's house. Her father was a practitioner of traditional Chinese medi-

---

1. There were nine levels of officialdom in the imperial Chinese court. My grandmother was a *sipin furen,* the wife of a fourth-level official.

cine. Her family lived in a one-story house in the eastern part of city. The house was dark, and I could barely see when I walked in from the outside, but I could see enough to be shocked. You could tell by looking at the interior of the house that her family was extremely poor. In my mind they were so impoverished that nothing in her family could possibly fall into any of the four forbidden categories.[2] In the search the only thing the Red Guards did take from her family was a package of *binpian*.[3]

The activities of that afternoon frightened me. If her poor family was unable to escape the attention of the Red Guards, mine was definitely on their list. The more I witnessed the Red Guards' actions, the more scared I became. If such innocent Chinese medicines were contraband against the Revolution, then a lot of things in my family could put us in danger. I became afraid that the Red Guards would search my family's house. Every day when I went home after school, I would stand trembling at the entrance of the street leading to my home, watching to see if anyone was there before I ran the rest of the way home.

My maternal grandfather had been a member of the Imperial Academy in the Qing dynasty. We had inherited some ancient things from him, things that held great sentimental value for our family. In some other settings of the city, these things had been labeled as elements of feudalism. I knew that we had a *dianshi* written by my grandfather at home.[4] I was afraid that if the Red Guards had found it, they would see it as *biantian zhang*.[5] I was so frightened by the Red Guards that I begged my *wai zu* and my mother to destroy it. But my *wai zu* said, "Baby, this is not *biantian zhang*. I promise. It's just a *dianshi*. Everyone likes to keep one or two things from their parents. We keep this for its

---

2. They were feudalism, capitalism, revisionism, and counterrevolution.

3. *Binpian*, or Borneo camphor, is a traditional Chinese medicine.

4. A *dianshi* was the final imperial examination, written by members of the Imperial Academy and presided over by the emperor. It was written on accordion-fold paper.

5. *Biantian zhang* were documents from the past that the Red Guards accused people of keeping in secret as reminders of their former glory, preserved in the eventuality of their return to power.

sentimental value." My *wai zu's* eyes welled up with tears. But I was crazy and would not listen to her. Almost daily I continued to insist that they burn it.

One afternoon when I came home from school, my *wai zu* held a family meeting. She said, "Your mother, aunt, and I have made a decision for the *dianshi*—burn it!" She paused for a moment, looking into my eyes. "I know you are frightened. We are going to destroy the *dianshi* for your sake, not because it is *biantian zhang*." All of us were crying.

My mother started a fire in the brazier. As the fire burned brighter and brighter, the flames were reflected in our faces, making them as red as the burning charcoal. My mother held the *dianshi* in her hands. But none of us had the courage to throw it into the fire. My mother looked at my aunt for help, but in vain. Finally my *wai zu* asked my mother to give her the *dianshi*. Before giving it to her, my mother tore a corner off the *dianshi*. The corner carried the Chinese characters for *huangshang* [emperor]) and *zaixia* [your subject]. My *wai zu* took the *dianshi* and immediately dropped it into the brazier. It turned to ashes in an instant. My *wai zu*, my aunt, and my mother were crying as though someone had died.

Logically, I know I was supposed to feel better or safer. But I didn't. I felt even more scared. My subconscious told me that I had done something terribly wrong. I began to apologize to my *wai zu*. She forgave me by saying, "You are so little and so scared. That's not your fault." My mother comforted me with the same words. Their forgiveness never eased the guilt I still carry in my heart.

In 1969, at the age of sixteen, I was sent to the Shengchan Jianshe Bintuan in Heilongjiang Province, northeast China.[6] In the corps I was chosen to be a member of the Mao Zedong Sixiang Xuanchuan Dui.[7]

---

6. This was the Production and Construction Corps. Under the control of the military, workers in these corps worked in the fields with peasants. They were paid for their labor but paid poorly.

7. This was the Propaganda Team for Mao Zedong Thought.

These teams toured various corps camps to perform revolutionary songs and dances.

There was one benefit to my being sent to the corps. I was able to make life a little easier for my family by sending them ten yuan on the first of each month from my monthly salary of thirty yuan.[8] One month I did not get my salary in time because we were touring so far from the headquarters of the corps. This meant a delay in the regular money I sent to my family. The next month I sent twenty yuan home to compensate. When she received the money, my mother wrote to me, "We are grateful for the money you send us each month, but it is still difficult when the money does not arrive on time. We hope you can continue to send it to us. We really appreciate your help." The letter made me feel so guilty I began sending twenty yuan to them each month. I wrote to my mother, "Please spend the extra ten yuan to buy some additional food for Wai Zu." My mother replied, "You only need send us ten yuan. When it arrives on time, we are able to manage a daily meal. You should not have given us twenty yuan because life for you over there is much tougher."

Every member of the Propaganda Team was required to keep Chairman Mao's thoughts in mind every minute of the day. Such work kept me physically and spiritually exhausted all the time.

In our performance the shorter members of the team would stand in the front rows holding portraits of Mao. The taller of us stood in the rear and carried drill rifles. I was the tallest member of the team.

One day my luck ran out. I do not remember why, but I was asked to hold Mao's portrait while carrying a rifle on my shoulder. That was my first time holding the portrait. It was a frightening experience. I felt like I was being assigned as a bodyguard for Mao. After the team leader told me about my new position and I left his office, Chinese characters started coming unbidden into my head. I could see them, one by one: *qiang* [gun], *bi* [kill]. *Qiang bi.* And then a sentence: *Qiang bi Mao zhu*

---

8. At the time, there were about three yuan to one dollar.

xi [Assassinate Chairman Mao]. I was terrified by these thoughts. I was afraid they would get me in the same trouble experienced by my high school Chinese teacher who was sentenced for thought crime. Her hair was cut in the *yin yang tou* style—half her head was shaved clean and the hair on the other half cut short like a man's.

I knew that if anyone learned what I was thinking, the Red Guards would shave my head like my teacher's. Everyone would know I was a thought criminal. I tried to hide my thoughts by forcing myself to think of the line "Mao Zedong's thought is great." But the harder I tried to think the "proper" thoughts, the more the other words returned.

I was too scared to perform. I could not control my mind or the shaking of my body. I was afraid that everyone already knew what I was thinking. I decided to confess to my team leader, a veteran of the Korean War. He was a kind man. He told me, "If this is the first time, it doesn't matter. You are just under too much stress. But if this happens again, I will have to report you."

As afraid as I was, the thoughts would not stay away. At the same time I could picture my hair cut *yin yang tou*. I knew that I could not bear the shame. I couldn't stand it at all. I told myself that no one would ever know if I didn't speak my thoughts out loud. But how could I hold them inside? They were too powerful. I decided that the only way out was suicide. The pressure of hiding my thoughts caused me to become sick, and I was granted special permission to go and see my doctor. I went home instead and spent the entire day cleaning up the house. I planned to kill myself by touching a bare electrical wire. I imagined that when my family found my body, they would think I was killed accidentally while cleaning house for them.

When everything was ready, I hesitated. I wanted to hear the voices of my family as they returned home. I especially wanted to hear the voice of my *wai zu* one last time. At the same time I was also afraid that if I heard them, I would change my mind. I went into the living room and opened the electrical panel there. There were so many wires. I was confused. Which wire or wires should I touch? If I picked the wrong ones, maybe it would not kill me, just cripple me. Life was so unfair. It wouldn't let me live properly, and it wouldn't let me die easily either. Suddenly I heard my *wai zu* coughing. I got even more nervous. I imagined that she wouldn't be able to live any longer if I died before her. I knew that I had to go on living for her sake. I ran out of the house to greet her, but there was no one there. I never told anyone in my family this story.

Before I attempted suicide, I burned all the letters from my family and my friends. One of the letters was from my *wai zu*. It was her only letter to me because her stroke in the park damaged her eyes and she could no longer hold a pen or brush. The letter, which was short, read, "My baby, I'm still alive. Don't you worry about me. Drink lots of water. Drinking a cup of water with a bit of salt every morning will help you. I need to see you again as pretty as you were."

I was eaten up by my sin: I forced my *wai zu* to burn the *dianshi* inherited from my grandfather, and then I burned my only letter from my *wai zu*. Maybe a few characters of the *dianshi* written by my grandfather still remained, but nothing remained of the letter from my *wai zu*.

Two days later I returned to my corps unit. A week or so later I received a letter from my mother that informed me that my *wai zu* was ill, but not in critical condition. In the letter my mother asked me to come home if possible. She was afraid that my *wai zu's* health might get worse. I was afraid to ask for leave again. I knew that the leader of the corps would criticize me as being bourgeois if I asked for another leave just because my *wai zu* was ill.

Two weeks later I received another telegram. It said, "Your mother is terminally ill. Come home immediately." I did not believe what this telegram said. I remembered a friend of mine was allowed to go home for a few days when her family sent her a telegram with a fake message saying that her mother was dying. I thought it must be that my *wai zu* was missing me and that my family was trying to get me to come home again. In those days the corps granted leaves of absence only to people whose immediate family members were terminally ill. This policy only covered parents and siblings. Visiting sick grandparents and other relatives was not allowed.

Nevertheless, I tried to go home. I went to our headquarters with the telegram in my hand. The team leader said that our Propaganda Team was about to stage a new performance, timed with a new political movement called Liang Yi Yi Pi.[9] His words made me feel ashamed of myself. I shouldn't even think about leaving when such important work was to be done. And the telegram wasn't even true. A person's political attitude was very important. I knew that if I wasn't careful and let my personal life get in the way of my political obligations, I might ruin my whole life. I decided to stay and concentrate on the new performance.

Another week passed and I went to the post office in town. Going there was the most pleasant part of life in the corps, especially when you got a letter or parcel from your family. As usual there was a letter waiting for me. I ran from the post office and opened the letter. The first line knocked me senseless. It said, "Your *wai zu* passed away last week. On her deathbed she constantly called your name. She tried to hold on until you could come home, but she wasn't strong enough." I wanted to cry and scream. I did not dare to do so in public, however. Tears were considered an expression of bourgeois feelings.

I felt my head swimming. I ran all the way down to the dormitory room that I shared with three other girls. Luckily for me, my roommates were not there. I cried myself to sleep. When I awoke I felt that something must have been wrong with the telegram I received a week ago. I went down to the post office and asked them for the original copy of the telegram. When I read it I saw that they had misread it as "mother dying." What it said was, "grandmother dying."

My *wai zu* was cremated, and her ashes were sprinkled in the river. All her life she liked to walk its banks. Whenever I miss her, I go to the river and talk to her. It was there that I told her how guilty I felt about burning her letter and bringing about the destruction of my grandfather's *dianshi*.

---

9. Liang Yi Yi Pi figuratively means "recall the people's suffering in the old society, voice the people's happiness in the new society, and criticize capitalism."

FOR A LITTLE LOVE

At five feet, six inches, Qiaoyu is tall for a Chinese female. Her height and dark skin make her stand out in the south, where most women are smaller and have delicate skin. Like the women in Gauguin's paintings from Tahiti, she is not beautiful but exotic.

She knows how to dress. Like most women in the city, Qiaoyu likes to be in style. At the interview she was wearing a black dress with red roses across the top, the red of the roses reflecting the color in her cheeks. Later that week I happened to see the dress in a department store. It cost the average monthly salary of someone like Qiaoyu.

Qiaoyu was a childhood friend. We were together in kindergarten. We went to different primary schools, but we still played together. When the Cultural Revolution started and my parents began to suffer political persecution and her parents were trying to avoid trouble, we stopped seeing each other. By the time the Cultural Revolution was over, we had grown apart.

One day after I had come to the United States, I received a letter with strangely familiar handwriting. I opened the envelope, and the first thing I read was the signature, Qiaoyu. It was more of a note than a letter, and it said, "Do you remember when we were in school and you edited that composition for me? I got 'Excellent' on that composition. I kept it for many years after, until the day I broke with my mother. Then I destroyed everything that could possibly remind me of the good times in my past—everything including that composition. Now I hear that you are writing a book. When you get home, come to see me."

When I returned to China, I went to visit Qiaoyu. She now works for an interior design company. In her Western-styled office, she introduced me to

her husband. There was no smile or pleasure on her face. He nodded to me
without standing up or offering to shake hands. He was clearly much older
than Qiaoyu and said nothing throughout our interview.

Qiaoyu was Gauguin's postimpressionist art, free and romantic. Her hus-
band was clearly the realist, reserved and conservative.

I asked Qiaoyu if she was happy.

"Don't you remember what you used to say all the time?" she replied.
"Nothing is good or bad;, only thinking makes it so."

My mother held the Chinese Communist Party as the highest moral
good in her life, even though she was not a Party member. For her there
was nothing beyond the Party's control or influence. Her biggest problem was that she was from a wealthy family. Her father was a rich rice
merchant and was executed by the Party in 1950. My mother was
twenty-one years old at the time. She had been trying to join the Party
ever since as a way of escaping her past. Her failure to get in and her un-
quenchable hope of joining meant that she would do anything for the
Party.

I never had much affection for my parents. I always admired girls in
the streets when they passed by hand in hand with their fathers or
mothers, an experience I never enjoyed.

My parents fought almost every day of my childhood. My mother
was a shrew. She ruled the household, constantly cursing and insulting
my father, who just accepted her abuse. Her word was law in our house.
My mother never smiled at me or my father or with us when we
laughed. I was deadly afraid of her. Since my father was so ill-treated, I
thought I had little right to complain about my fate. From the time I
started kindergarten, my father took me to school at the start of each
week, returning to pick me up for the weekend. But my relationship
with him was little better than his or mine with my mother. He was too
weak for me to admire.

I was only nine years old when the Cultural Revolution broke out in
1966. My father and mother escaped the political persecution of many
of their intellectual colleagues and friends. Perhaps they escaped the ter-

ror because they were not important, well-known writers. They dreamed of being Party members. Membership offered them more chances for promotion. They spent their time trying to ingratiate themselves with Party bureaucrats, to little avail. They were not allowed into the Party. Never ones to give up hope, they engaged themselves in the Revolution in a fanatical fashion.

I only remember one affectionate moment between my parents. One New Year's Day my father put a sheet of white paper on his desk and wrote with a brush in his hand while my mother dictated to him. They were writing a *da zi bao*—a big-character poster about one of their colleagues. I never saw them more affectionate or cooperative. It was the only time I ever saw them close to each other without fighting or quarreling. I noticed that because they were so zealous and devoted, they did not see me watching them.

My parents treated me as though I was a burden taking up their time and energy. They wanted no one questioning their loyalty to the Revolution or to the Party. In their quest for Party favors, they left me anywhere: my grandmother's home, my aunt's home, or the homes of other relatives. I remember being kicked out of my aunt's house for getting sick on green grapes from the grapevines next door. My aunt accused me of setting a bad example for her children, who were several years older than me, and who had fed me the grapes.

The year after the Cultural Revolution started, after many such incidents at various relatives' houses, my mother sent me to live with her brother, more than one thousand miles away. I stayed in my uncle's house for three years. During this period, my mother never once wrote to me. She maintained businesslike contacts with my uncle, sending him my monthly living expenses as though she was paying a storage fee. My uncle treated me like an indentured servant. He did not talk to me except to order me around, just like the rest of the members of his family. I suppose he thought his responsibility to me was just to keep me alive until my mother would allow me to return home.

My aunt was worse. At every meal she would accuse me of eating too much and working too little. I was afraid to take more than one bowl of rice. She would say humiliating things like, "How could you have the face to eat at this table? Your parents do not give us enough money to feed such a pig." When the money my mother sent to them was one or two days late, she would not feed me at all. I would steal food from the kitchen at night, fearing for my life.

My jobs around the house included watching my younger cousin, a troublesome boy of five; cleaning the house; washing the family clothes; and frequently cooking meals for the whole family. This saved my aunt and uncle the cost of a live-in maid.

I felt wronged. I wanted to write to my father and my mother to tell them what life was like, but my uncle refused to tell me their mailing address. One day when everyone was gone, I searched my uncle's desk. I found my parent's address and wrote it on a scrap of paper. Since I didn't know how to write many Chinese characters and those I did know wouldn't be useful, I wrote only one line: "Dear Daddy and Mom, Please take me home. I will be a good child."

When I finished the letter, I realized that I had neither a stamp nor the money to buy one. I had to wait a month until my mother sent money to my uncle. Although my mother sent thirty yuan [about ten dollars] to my uncle every month, he gave me an allowance of only one jiao (equivalent to two cents). Sending my parents that letter meant that I would not have any of the inexpensive treats I enjoyed once a month: no popsicles or popcorn. Nor would I have anything new to read. Each month when I got my allowance, I rented one book from the local bookstore. Since all the schools in the country were closed by the Cultural Revolution in accordance with the Party's calling—"Suspending classes to make revolution"—I couldn't go to school. The bookstore was my favorite place.

I spent my whole month's allowance on the stamp to send that letter. I was excited with the idea that my mother would bring me home soon. About three weeks later my aunt, my uncle's wife, came home with my letter. She gave me a bad look, throwing the letter on the dining table and yelling at me; "How dare you write your parents! How dare you accuse us of treating you badly! Luckily for us you don't even know how to address a letter. You are so stupid!"

Laughing, she walked away, leaving the opened letter on the table. I picked it up and saw my own handwriting, the stamp that cost me so much, with the butterfly printed on it. I was confused. How had this terrible woman gotten my letter? I didn't dare ask. That night after dinner my older cousin laughed at me. I learned that I had put my own address in the middle of the envelope where the recipient's address should have gone. I put my mother's address in the return address spot.

After three years of being enslaved in my uncle's household, and in time for high school, I was sent home by my uncle because I caught pneumonia. He refused to pay for my medical care. Now whenever I think of them, they remind me of evil capitalists in children's books who squeezed blood from their child laborers.

If my parents had only ignored me, I might have forgiven them. What I cannot forgive is their willingness to sacrifice my life in their pursuit of Party membership.

When I returned home, my parents enrolled me in a local vocational high school as a way of keeping me out of the house. When I graduated, I was assigned to work in a local automobile repair and spare parts factory. However, I refused to go to work there because I wanted to take the entrance exam for the Central Conservatory of Music in Beijing. It had always been my dream to be a singer. Going to work at the factory meant giving up my dreams. There would be no time to study or practice my music.

In those days the government had a policy that no vocational workers would be allowed to take the entrance exam for college or university until they had completed two years of service for the government. When I refused to take the job at the factory, I both was unemployed and had little hope of finding a job. Without a job, there was no way for me to do the required service for the government. My mother wrote for a literature magazine, and her boss was her editor. Ever eager to keep me busy, my mother asked for help from the chief editor at the magazine where she worked. Her boss hired me as a temporary secretary.

This man, Tang Xing, was a celebrated literary critic. He was a friend of my parents and lived in the same compound as my family. As a high school student, I had frequently visited him, asking his help with my writing. I couldn't ask for help from my father or mother even though they were both writers. The wife of the literary critic was a professor of physics. She frequently helped me with my math homework.

One night in the summer of 1978, after I had been working for the magazine for just two months, I went the critic's house for help with my writing. His wife and children were not at home. He seated me at his desk, but instead of sitting beside me, as he usually did, he stood behind me. I could feel his breath on the back of my neck. I moved a bit and turned my head. I found he was staring down my blouse and not reading my assignment. All of a sudden he kissed the back of my neck. I was completely shocked—then nervous. He was the first person who ever kissed me. Neither my mother nor my father ever kissed or hugged me. I was so innocent and naive that I worried his kisses might make me pregnant. But at the same time his attention was desirable.

Before I was could recover from the shock, he started flattering me. "It's not my fault I want to kiss you. It's your fault. How could I not be carried away by such beauty?"

My mother had often told me I was ugly and stupid. No one had ever told me I was desirable or pretty. I was vulnerable to this new attention. If I would have held back my feelings a little bit, my whole life today would be different, but I didn't. I just let my feelings run.

The next day I came into his office many times. It was as if a lodestone was drawing my body there. He shared the office with the chief editor of the magazine. I could not say anything private to him. It seemed that he and I had a tacit mutual understanding on this point. He just smiled at me gently. I was satisfied; my heart was full of peace and quiet. I was the happiest girl in the world. Naively, I thought this was what romance was all about.

On the morning of the fourth day of our love, as I was about to leave for work, my mother stopped me. "You are not to go to work anymore," she said. She did not go to work either but stayed at home to watch me. It was horrible. She refused to tell me why I was not allowed to go, nor did she explain why she kept watch over me.

I knew that my mother smelled something unusual between me and Tang Xing, but she could not prove it. Keeping me at home was her strategy for finding out what was going on. My only protection was to act normally. The first day there was no problem, but by the second day there was no way for me to continue to act normally. I was full of nervous energy. I paced in my room, back and forth.

Through the window of my bedroom I could see the window of Tang Xing's study and the courtyard of his house. When he left home for his office and when he returned, I was standing by my window, watching. That was my only chance to see him. He never glanced my way, but I was certain he knew I was standing by my window. At night I did not switch off my light until his was off. I imagined that he was thinking of me by his desk, where we began our love. I imagined that he was suffering the bitterness of stifled love. I couldn't go to bed til his study sat in darkness.

My mother kept me locked in the house for a week. Then on Sunday she said, "I'm taking you to the People's Park today." This was strange because she had never taken me anyplace before, even as a little girl. On hearing this I was not pleased; instead I became more nervous. I knew this was just another one of her tricks.

When we got the park, I saw my father and another woman, a Party political writer from the magazine where he worked. They were waiting for us at the main gate. My mother led all of us to a teahouse in the park. We sat with our tea for a while, my father and the writer talking about local politics. Then without warning my father said, "Well, I think we'll walk around the park a bit. Do you want to join us?"

"No, you two go ahead," answered my mother. Actually I wanted to go with them to escape my mother. But I didn't dare say so.

My mother watched my father and the writer as they walked away. She looked into my eyes without speaking for a moment and then said, "Your father and I realize that we haven't done enough for you in the past. We wanted to take you out today to show our concern for you."

I was laughing in my heart. I was not touched at all. I was totally numb. "It's too late for you to care for me now," I thought. "My childhood has gone. Where were you when I needed your love and attention?"

All my experiences of being left with relatives while my parents participated in the "Great Socialist Class Struggle" flashed through my mind while my mother made her phony attempts at motherly talk. Timing really was everything. Even if my mother was sincere, which I doubted, it was just too late. My heart was dead, and any chance we had for love was lost.

"This society is complicated. You cannot tell good people from bad," my mother said.

"That's ridiculous," I thought, "trying to tell me how to distinguish good from bad when I have grown up." I didn't answer, hoping she would take my silence as a sign of daughterly obedience. She didn't. Without any warning in her face, she turned on me.

"Confess! What kind of relationship do you have with Tang Xing? How deeply are you involved with him? For you own good you had better tell me everything."

I remained silent. How could I tell her anything? She had never opened her heart to me. Moreover, this man was the only person in this world who had ever shown me warmth and tender feelings.

My silence angered her and in a strident voice she said, "We will take you to the hospital and have a doctor look at you. Then we will know, you honorless creature!"

Her shouting attracted the attention of the people in the teahouse. At this moment my father and the writer came back. The woman was a member of the Party committee of the magazine. My mother had brought her along so she could see how loyal my mother was to the Party.

"You'd better tell your mother the truth," the writer said. "We're only doing this for your own good."

Since my mother did not get what she expected from me, the next day the secretary of the Party committee and two other members came to my home. The secretary, Li, told me that they needed to ask me some questions about Tang Xing on behalf of the Party committee. My mother went to her bedroom, and my father went into his office.

I do not remember exactly what secretary Li said to me that day, but the point of the conversation was clear. He advised me to establish a great revolutionary goal. He told me that I was still young and unable to distinguish good from bad. He said, "You shouldn't allow something as insignificant as love to spoil your future. All you need to do is to tell us what the man did to you. If you tell us the truth, we won't trouble you. I promise."

At this time the only thing I had heard from Tang Xing was a note asking me to be quiet. He told me that my mother and her friends only wanted to stir a scandal around him and ruin his career. He said that they were jealous of his talent, of which they had little or none.

I said nothing to secretary Li and the two members of the committee. My mother learned that not even a secretary of the Party could open my mouth. That night, frustrated by my silence, she locked me and herself inside my bedroom, so my father couldn't come in and stop her. Then she beat me as hard as she could with a stick. The only reaction I had was to turn my back to her when she tried to hit my face. I was so silly. I tried to protect my face for Tang Xing because he had praised my beauty and because he was the first person to kiss me. Throughout the beating, my mother accused me of being a shameless whore.

My mother did not stop the beating until my back was covered with bruises and she was completely exhausted. Then she retired to her bedroom. I opened my photo album. I took out all the pictures of my mother and tore them to pieces. Then I cleaned my face and teeth, put on clean clothes, and slipped out of the house.

Once I was in the street, I realized that I had no place to go. One thing I was certain of was that I wanted to leave my mother as far behind as possible. I walked west, which led me as far from home as fast as possible. I was sad and tired. I kept thinking of Tang Xing. I missed his arms. I thought, if I can get to him, I can have peace and love. But I was unable to reach him. Like most homes in China, there was no telephone at his home. I wandered through the city until I reached the People's Park, where I fell asleep on the grass.

I waited until midmorning, when I could be sure that he was in his office; then I called his office from a phone booth. I told him that I had left home last night and asked him for help. He said he would meet me at the gate of the park soon.

I was standing at the main entrance of the park when Tang Xing arrived, riding an old black bicycle. I greeted him by touching his arm. He responded by dragging me under a parasol tree where we could talk unnoticed.

The touch of his hand was so welcome that I naturally closed my eyes and opened my mouth. Then I heard a strange voice in my ears.

"I cannot help you," he said. "Go back to your mother."

It sounded like thunder rolling over my head. I thought, whose voice is this? What words are these? I opened my eyes. In front of me was the man I loved and counted on so much. Then I realized that there was something more important for him than me—his social status, his reputation, his career.

"If you really love me, you should think about me," he said.

I looked at him, not knowing what I should say or could say to him. He took me to the park office. He told the ranger that I had a fight with my mother and he happened to meet me at the park. He asked the ranger for a cup of water for me and said that he would inform my mother. The two of them left me. I never saw Tang Xing again.

Later on another writer told me that Tang Xing had written a report to the Party committee of the magazine the day he left me at the park. He accused me of trying to trade my body for a permanent job at the magazine. He described me as an evil, immoral woman. His wife supported his claims. She swore to the Party committee that her husband and I had no personal relationship. She even claimed that I had tried to seduce Tang Xing.

There is an old Chinese curse that says, "Give the dog an ill name and hang him." I now have the reputation as a sly dog, a reputation that hangs me every day of my life.

Tang Xing betrayed me in the autumn of 1978. Since that day my mother has not talked to me. It is as though we are not even related. Nineteen seventy-eight was also the year I turned twenty-one. History has its own ways of repeating itself. My mother escaped the shadow of her family and became a communist at the age of twenty-one. At that same age I escaped from her. The difference was that I would never believe in anything or anyone ever again.

The woman who gave me life was such a mean woman, and the man who inspired my first love was such a selfish one. My mother thought I threatened her chances for joining the Party, so she sent me away at an early age. She thought she could get ahead at the magazine, so she exposed my relationship with her boss to the Party committee. Tang Xing put the blame on me for my mother's actions, choosing to believe that I wanted to spoil his future. Everyone who could have loved me and should have loved me abandoned me, physically, spiritually, and emotionally.

After the disaster my mother refused to admit to anyone that I was her daughter. She also forbade my father to claim me. She even forbade my father to mention my name in front of her. I had some sympathy for my father. When I was young, he remained married to my mother for my sake, even though it meant that his career might suffer because of her parents. But I don't have a lot of sympathy for him because, now that I am grown, he stays married to my mother. He claims that they are old and need each other's company.

I got married one year ago last month. My parents did not come to the wedding. My mother rejected my invitation and prevented my father from coming. Later he had a serious fight with my mother. He warned her, "If you don't want to claim her as your daughter, that's your right. But she is my only child. You can't stop me from seeing her."

To the best of my knowledge, that was the first time my father ever stood up for himself. Since the wedding my mother has relented and allows him to visit me once in a while. Perhaps it was because she is getting old and is afraid my father will leave her and come to live with me.

Despite all my problems with my mother, I continued to try to get her to love me. I married my husband to please my father and because I was tired and scared by the scandal. Within the first year of my marriage, I was pregnant and gave birth to my son. I thought he would make it possible for me to go back to my family.

On the day he was six months old, I took my son to my parents' house. There are two houses in the compound where my parents live. My father and I were playing with my son in front of the house across the courtyard from my parents' house. Because my mother did not know I had a child, my father thought it might be the right time to show her her grandson. He took the baby into their house while I waited outside.

A few minutes later I heard my son screaming loudly, as though someone was stepping on his chest. I rushed into my parents' house. My son was lying on the concrete floor on his back. I picked him up and discovered bruises on his soft head.

My father told me that at first my mother seemed to be happy to see the baby. She teased him and tickled him as my father held him. Then she wanted to hold him, so my father handed him over to her. She tickled him some more and kissed him on the cheek. My son was smiling at her and making happy sounds.

Finally she asked my father, "Whose child is this?"

"This is your daughter's son," my father said.

As soon as she heard this, my mother dropped my son on the ground. Then she walked away. Holding him in my arms, my heart sank. I felt terribly sorry for my son. He was such a little thing. He had done nothing. My mother had simply shifted her anger from me to my son. Then I cried. I did not cry when my mother beat me up. I did not cry when Tang Xing betrayed me. But I cried for my son. When I calmed down, I realized that nothing was really unfair for my son. I would not abuse him or abandon him. I knew better.

SUSTAINING LIFE

*W*uxin *says that three things are important to making a gentleman: nice skin, an elegant manner, and classical dress. Wuxin has the delicate skin that many women dream of having. He has been using men's facial cream made of pearls for years.*[1] *He always dresses nicely. On the day we met to talk, he looked quite dapper. He was wearing a sharp, french-cuff white shirt tucked into pressed navy trousers; a black alligator belt, and tan English loafers. He buys his clothing from the Gold Lion in Hong Kong. He says he does not trust merchandise with the "Made in China" labels.*

Wuxin is the manager of an import-export company in Chongqing. He is divorced from his first wife, a schoolteacher, and is now married to a Party official's daughter. Friends say that he is indifferent to his second wife and married her because of her father's connections, which got him his present job. When we met for the interview, I chided him about his reputation. He retorted, "I'm forty-five years old. I don't need anyone to tell me what is moral. Ever since Wenge this world has been upside down.[2] *Look at my father, dead spirit, dead soul. Ask him about morality and justice."*

It was the twenty-fifth of January 1967. I remember it as clearly as today. What a day. We lived on campus at an agricultural college in a suburb of Chengdu. My father taught classes in Chinese language and culture.

---

1. The Chinese believe that pearls can clarify and smooth the skin.
2. Wenge is an abbreviated term for the Cultural Revolution.

Around seven o'clock that morning I went to the canteen to buy breakfast. My mother passed away during the great famine in 1963, and since that time my father and I depended on the college canteen for our meals. I was only gone about fifteen minutes, but in that short period of time my whole world would be turned upside down. When I returned, the door and the windows to the house were covered with big-character posters that read; "Expose the Historical Reactionary Wu Yang! Down with the Capitalist Academic Authority Wu Yang!" Wu Yang was my father's name, and every place it was written on the posters was crossed out with red ink.

I dashed into the house, afraid my father had been taken away by the Red Guards. He was standing in the center of the living room, shaking like a person suffering from malaria. We glanced at each other silently for a second. Then my father looked away, staring at his feet. He looked scared, puzzled, and guilty all at the same time.

I urged him to come to the table and eat breakfast. Before we could sit down, six young guards in their twenties walked into the house. They all had guns. One of them, a young woman, looked familiar, but I couldn't place her until she shouted in the voice I had heard many times reading her poetry to my father. She wrote beautiful Chinese poetry in the classical style and had been my father's favorite student.

I remembered her with two long braids in her hair, one over her right shoulder and the other down her back. They would dance as she walked. The long-haired poet was gone. Her hair had been cut short like a boy's—revolutionary chic. She wore a brown military belt over a yellow jacket. She rested her right hand on her pistol holster, while waving her left hand in the air and shouting at her comrades, "You five stay outside to block the way in case this old reactionary tries to escape."

Her familiar voice shocked my father more than the Rebels' accusations that he was a reactionary. "Li Yang," my father said, "you should be in the classroom studying."

"Shut up, you reactionary!" Li Yang shouted back at my father. Then she ordered her followers to search our house. They turned it inside out.

They took all our books, original paintings, clothes, and our savings book.

"These are proof of your counterrevolutionary past," Li Yang said, pointing at our family treasures. Searching through the pile of about-to-be confiscated goods, she singled out one book, covered in the butcher paper my father used to protect his more valuable books. She tossed the book on the dining room table in front of my father, saying, "This is the only thing you need. Study it."

She headed out of the house, followed by her comrades.

The house was very quiet. For a moment neither my father nor I moved. We just looked at each other, then glanced around the house as if to make sure no one was hiding there. "Have they really left?" my father asked. He picked up the book and opened it. I could see the title over his shoulder, *Mao Zedong on Education.* My father turned to the portrait of Mao on the front page.

"Chairman Mao, Chairman Mao," he said. "I have done what you required. Tell me, what did I do wrong? Now my students rebel against their teachers."

The Rebels left us locked in our house. I guess they were afraid that we might flee. About one o'clock in the afternoon Li Yang came again with four young men. They tied my father's hands behind his back and then mine. They took us through quiet streets to a crowded meeting hall at the college. As we were led down the aisle, the crowd shouted in one voice, "Down with the reactionary Wu Yang!" As soon as the crowd's shouting quieted, I shouted in return, "My father is not a reactionary."

"If you shout again, I will see to it that you wear the label of reactionary forever." Li Yang pushed down on my neck. "Don't test me. Your youth will not protect you." I was frightened. The two of us were pulled up the stairs to the platform where my father had lectured for many years. I stood quietly beside my father as we suffered through two hours of denunciation and criticism. The humiliation ended with Li Yang's statement, "I declare on behalf of the revolutionary masses that I will send this old reactionary and his young son to the countryside for labor reform."

Three Red Guards escorted my father and me to the railway station. Two days later we were taken off the train outside a city in northern China. We spent the entire next day on a bus that took us to a Red Flag commune far into the mountains. Outside the bus station there were five bored peasants, leaning on muddy bicycles, waiting for us. One of the three Red Guards pointed to two peasants and ordered, "You two load up these two reactionaries." One peasant turned to my father and said, "Can you jump on the bicycle while I ride?"

"Yes, yes," my father nodded like a chicken picking up rice from the ground. I knew he was trying to be cooperative, but he had never ridden on a bicycle in his life. It took him four tries to get up onto the rack on the back of the bicycle. Once he was up and going, the three Red Guards and I jumped on the backs of the remaining bicycles.

The peasant hauling my father took the lead, my bicycle came next, and our guards brought up the rear. That countryside road was full of holes. The Red Guards and I all held onto the waist of our chauffeur, but not my father. I guess he dared not hold on because he had been denounced as a reactionary.

It was evening when we arrived in the village. The three Red Guards were treated to dinner, while my father and I were sent to the meeting hall in the village to await more denunciation and criticism from the villagers.

We waited and waited. Some of the children from the village stuck their dirty faces through the crack of the door and stared at us. They fled like birds when their parents yelled at them. My father stared fixedly at the corner. Following his gaze, I saw a large spider weaving a web in the corner. I picked up a chunk of dirt and threw it at the spider. It broke the web, but the spider still hung there. My father sighed and said, "We are like that spider now."

My stomach was rumbling. I was starving when the three Rebels walked in, accompanied by a man with weathered face. "I'm sorry, so sorry. You revolutionary young pathbreakers will have to take these two reactionaries to some other place for labor reform. The work here is too light to properly reform them."

What the man was really saying was that he did not want to take us because he was already trying to support a large population on poor land but that he did not dare speak directly. To do so would be to run the risk of being labeled a counterrevolutionary.

We left in the morning and traveled another three days before we arrived at another Red Flag commune in southwestern China. The people's communes worked under a labor point system that was used to ration food. The more points a commune member earned, the better he or she ate. A male laborer could earn as many as ten points per day; a female could earn eight. Because we were reactionaries and the targets of the proletarian dictatorship, my father could earn only five points a day and I, three points. Regardless of how long or hard we worked, in the fifteen years I was in that village, we never had enough to eat.

Soon the starvation began to show in my father's health. His whole body began to swell up. If I touched him, the place I pushed would form a dimple. When I released my touch, the dimple remained. It was kind of like bread. When you poke at a loaf of bread, the place you touch does not pop back out. My father's body acted the same way. Even our wok became rusty from not being used regularly. Starving was such a horrible experience. It was worse than the witch-hunt, criticism, and denunciation that got us sent to the countryside in the first place.

I watched my father getting more and more frail as time went by. Most nights we went to bed without eating anything. The local peasants liked to say, "Well-fed people are lazy and sleep all the time. Starving them keeps them awake." It was absolutely true. Many nights I could not fall asleep and lay there listening to my father sigh.

One night I had a dream about fighting with someone over a potato. Now fighting over a delicious pork dinner would be worthwhile, but fighting over a potato? What an impoverished dream life we had. All of a sudden I heard a heartbreaking scream. I thought I was still dreaming. Then another scream. It sounded like someone was being killed. I woke up this time. It was my father.

I was so tired that I could not even get up. Lying in my bed, I asked my father, "Why are you screaming?"

"It's nothing. You were dreaming," my father said in a weak voice. "Did I wake you?"

I didn't say anything and fell asleep again. Soon I started dreaming about food again.

When I got up the next morning something was strange. Usually my father was out of bed early in the morning. This morning he was still in bed, even when I was ready to go to work in the fields. I became nervous and went over to see if he was okay. His pillow was soaked in blood, and his face was a dark red mask of dried blood. I shook him awake. "Dad, Dad." He opened his eyes but shut them again at once. I held his head in my hands, demanding that he awaken. "Don't leave me alone, Dad," I said. There was a wan smile on his face when my hand felt something wrong with his head. I took a close look at the left side of his head. There was no ear, only the veins.

"Your ear. Where is your ear, Dad?" I shook him.

"A rat ate it," my father said weakly. Then I remembered the horrible screaming. It was then that the rat was gnawing my father's ear. He was so frail that he did not have the strength to chase it away.

"You see, Son, even the rats take advantage of us," my father said. He had never said anything so depressing and pessimistic. I felt like it was the end of the world, but I told my father, "Hang on, Dad. I'm going to find a doctor."

I knew that we did not have money for a doctor, so I went to the Taoist priest Wang, who lived at the other end of the village. He had some mastery of traditional Chinese medicine, learned when he was practicing Taoism in the mountains. Wang was no longer a practicing priest because the Cultural Revolution had declared Taoism to be one of the Four Olds. Priest or not, the peasants still addressed him as Wang Taoshi [Father or Priest] and would go to see him when they needed medical attention.

I knocked at his door and then kneeled as he came out. I told him our story. "Please save my father, Wang Taoshi," I begged.

The old Taoist pulled me up and said, "Even the mice are hungry these days, but usually they only attack the diseased. Your father is seriously ill. It would be impossible to treat him only with medicine. He needs to take some tonic and eat nourishing foods to build up his health."

Wang gave me a small jar of herbal medicine he made in his backyard. The medicine would cure my father's wounded head, he said, but not restore his health. I was afraid his other ear might be taken if I could not get him some food. The problem was money—there was no way to get any. The people who had good hearts, like Wang Taoshi, were just as poor as us. People with money would not lend it to us for political reasons.

I begged the leadership of the commune to lend us some grain against our next year's grain distribution. I told them, "I don't care that you labeled my father a counterrevolutionary. He is dying of starvation. He has to have enough to eat if he is going to reform himself."

The leaders refused me. One of them, a young man in his twenties, told me, "Your father lived a luxurious life before the liberation, serving the KMT. How dare you stand up for that old reactionary? You say he is dying of starvation? He deserves it. So do you, you little reactionary."

However, I made up my mind to get some food for my father no matter what. An idea crossed my mind.

The local peasants were very superstitious. They believed that demons have an intangible spirit power that affects the life of individuals. They believe that when a person is sick, their soul is capable of slipping out of the body and wandering about. Demons can frighten a soul away or steal the soul from the body. Diseases and other calamities may result. Once the soul is taken, the patient is believed to be possessed by demons, which must be exorcised by a shaman.

The Cultural Revolution did away with the shamans' practices—they were "elements against the socialist spirit of the revolution." The rites that they practiced to chase out demons and call back the soul disappeared along with the shamans. However, the peasants still held their beliefs and were still in awe of the power of the demons. Whenever someone was ill, family members would toss their best food into a "sacred" valley.

The next day I heard that the son of the Party's secretary of the brigade had been sick with a fever for several days. The secretary's wife was so worried about her son that she had been asking to borrow food from everyone. When she did not come to transplant rice shoots in the field that day, I knew she was at home preparing sacrificial food for the demons.

Male laborers do not do rice transplanting because it demands a continuous bending movement. Local custom had it that women had waists and men did not. Therefore, men were unable to bend over and work. Male laborers were responsible for transporting the rice seedlings to the fields from the greenhouse. The third trip we made to get seedlings, I slipped down the road leading to the Party secretary's house.

I hid in some bushes across from the house, waiting for the secretary's wife. Soon she appeared carrying a bamboo basket. She looked around to see if anyone was watching her; then she walked quickly toward the west. I followed her to the sacred valley. Several times she took something from the basket and tossed it into the bushes. Then she headed home, sprinkling raw rice on the road and calling, "Er-zi ah [Son] come home, come home."

As soon as she disappeared, I walked down into the valley. She had offered the demons boiled eggs, colored red. I collected them all. Ten in total. At the moment I felt like I had found a huge gold bar or something equally valuable.

I rushed home and presented the eggs to my father. He refused to eat them, however, asking instead where they had come from. He knew we could not afford anything as luxurious as eggs.

"The eggs are from Wang Taoshi," I said. I had to tell him a white lie because he would rather starve than sacrifice his dignity and eat stolen food.

"Why are they colored red?" he asked.

"They were left over from one of Wang Taoshi's rites," I murmured.

Satisfied, he began to eat. He made me promise to not accept ritual food from anyone in the future. "Sacrificial offerings to deities and ancestors are from the Four Olds. The Party said so," he said.

That didn't stop me from going to the valley the next day, where I found more eggs. That poor woman must have thought the demons accepted her offering. I wouldn't have stolen her offerings if her husband, the representative of the Party, had showed a bit of sympathy for my father and treated him like a human being.

A PROPER LADY

Wanjia is a civil engineer in Beijing. Her parents and mine are old friends, so I stayed with them during the summer of 1991.

She is about five feet tall and a bit on the chubby side. However, her body's imperfections never seem to bother her, nor do they seem to distract men. She always has a cluster of male friends surrounding her. When asked about her crowd of admirers, she laughs and says, "That's what my mother says, 'Who are all those boys, and what are you doing with them?'" Like her parents, Wanjia does not know what attracts men to her, but she clearly likes the attention.

As intellectuals, her parents have certain expectations of a future husband for their daughter. Under the Confucian morality of China's intellectual classes, her husband should be an intellectual. A few years ago, Wanjia was in love with a nice young man who was a student in Qinghua University (the MIT of China). He was acceptable husband material until the day he quit the university to go to work in a Sino-American joint venture company, where he will likely earn triple the monthly salary of a couple of senior intellectuals combined.

Wanjia's mother gave the poor young man a two-hour lecture, berating him for his career move. Her mother's attitude convinced Wanjia to marry the man soon thereafter. When asked by her mother how she could marry a businessman, she answered, "I don't want to be the proper lady you expect me to be."

I wanted to ask her if she loved her husband, but I knew that I would not get a satisfactory answer to such a trite question. But I did get an answer when she talked about her ideas about relationships between men and women. Women, she said, long for an assured livelihood from the men they *love. But a woman should not let a man occupy her whole life. She has to have her own emotions and thoughts. What she decides to do should be based on her own thoughts and not on the existence of someone else. Only in this way can a woman not live in a man's shadow.*

Wanjia thinks that it is satisfying for a woman to love one man, but for most men, one woman cannot make them content. On this point, if a woman is not open-minded and magnanimous, if she is too devoted to one man, she is likely to suffer. Therefore, men and women should have some distance in their relationships, some ambiguity.

What Wanjia said is too profound to match her doll-like face, round eyes with long eyelashes, and little, round mouth with tiny teeth. It is the sharp contrast between her thoughtful mind and her innocent face that makes her so charming to so many young men, and this charm masks her less than perfect body.

Whenever I see teenagers nowadays, so free to make friends with the opposite sex, one experience out of my past returns to my mind. The years pass, but what happened to me as a child still haunts me. The scar it left will not go away.

It was 1976. The Cultural Revolution had started to wind down. I was at a junior high school located in the northern part of Beijing. I was unique at the school because of my intellectual background. My mother was a senior editor for the city's largest magazine, and my father was a well-known professor in the field of international economics. I was among the intellectual minority at the junior high, where working-class kids made up about 80 percent of the student body. When school was over each day, all the boys gathered at the gate of the school and harassed the prettier girls. Those boys acted like little hooligans. I was always scared to pass them. I had been harassed a couple of times, but I did not have courage to tell my parents or my teachers. I knew that they would think of me as a bad girl. In China, especially during the Cultural Revolution, anything that happened to a girl was her own fault because her loose behavior caused the trouble. For a time I believed this.

During the spring of each year, we students were sent to the country-side to do fieldwork with the peasants for one month. I was assigned to work at the canteen because I was too small to do the heavy work in the fields. There was a boy, Liu Bin, from another class who was also as-signed to work in the canteen. I had heard that he was popular with the girls. This boy and I were always assigned to the same shift, but we never talked to each other. One day I felt there was something different in his eyes when he looked at me.

This was something I had not experienced before. I had read love scenes in forbidden books like *Gone with the Wind* and *Anna Karenina.* Now I felt like I subconsciously understood something from the expres-sion in the eyes of this boy. This was frightening because these feelings between women and men were considered extremely bad.

Three days after we returned to school, this boy cut in front of me riding a bicycle. I felt myself blush immediately, and my heart was up in my throat. He put a letter in my hand and quickly rode away without saying a word. I looked around to make sure no one saw us. Then I put the letter into my schoolbag and ran all the way back home, where I went into the bathroom and opened the letter. It was short, only two sentences. He said that after working with me in the canteen, he liked me and he wanted to make friends with me. The first thing that crossed my mind was that I was a bad girl for reading the letter. I was shaking and had no idea what I was supposed to do with the letter. The next day I returned the letter to him in the corridor at school. He wrote me an-other letter the next day. I returned it to him unopened.

He continued to bother me for a couple of weeks and then he stopped. I was relieved and thought everything was okay. Then one day when I came home from school, no one was home. My parents did not come back until late. They looked unhappy. Cautiously I asked them what was wrong. My mother burst out, yelling at me, "What have you been doing behind our backs? You must tell us everything that hap-pened between you and that little hooligan!" It was a hail of bullets. "Confess! You confess!" my mother screamed. I remained silent.

From their accusations I learned that my parents had come from the principal's office at school. The principal told them that the boy's father had found the two letters Liu Bin had written to me. The father was almost illiterate and could not understand everything his son had written, so he took the letters to the school. He told the principal that he believed his son was being seduced by a bad girl. The principal was an ultraleftist who decided that he had encountered a dangerous evil. He called my parents to his office to give them a moral and political lecture.

The next day my mother took me to the principal. She told me that what she was doing was for my own good. After a long lecture on morality, the principal sent me to the teacher in charge of my class. The teacher took me to his office. He asked me to tell him the way that Liu Bin and I used to communicate with each other.

When he heard my side of the story, he told me that he was dubious and that he did not know if he believed what I said. The whole time I was talking to him, he held my hands and rubbed them back and forth. The way he looked at me was dirty. I was scared and confused, but I dared not pull my hands away. I thought he was the only person who could prove my innocence. Teachers have such authority in China.

After listening to me and lecturing me for more than an hour, while he continued to hold my hands, my teacher promised he would not tell anybody what I had done. Then I figured out that he, too, believed I was a bad girl. I had done nothing, yet I was unable to get anyone to believe me.

My teacher told me not to return to school until I had written a confession. A few days latter I handed in my "confession." I strongly criticized myself, saying I had been seduced by the bad influences of a bourgeois lifestyle. I said that from then on, I would concentrate on studying for the Revolution. Then the teacher told me my case was dismissed, and he forgave me because I was an *A* student.

However, as far as the rest of the world went, it was, and is, not over at all. At school all the teachers gave me bad looks out of the corner of their eyes. They all used me as an example to their students. The teach-

ers in my classes would call me to their offices and lecture me frequently. They repeatedly told me that because I had made a serious mistake, I would be required to pay extra careful attention to myself. They
all promised me they would not tell anyone, but it was apparent that everyone was going to give me a lecture. They all used the same for-
mula—because I had once been bad, I would always have to be extra
good. At home my parents were extremely strict with me and watched
over every single movement I made. My parents set a time when I had
to be home from school, and I was not allowed to be out of the house
afterward.

Two years later I transferred to another school because my family had
moved to the eastern part of the city. At the new school the teachers still
gave me a lecture once in a while, implying I had done something
wrong in my past, and warned me to behave myself. They all made me
feel guilty and kept me believing that I was bad.

One day as I left school in a pouring rain, I saw a young man standing
in front of the store across the street. He did not have an umbrella, and
he was thoroughly soaked. It was Liu Bin. He waved to me when he saw
me. I pretended not to see him. I was afraid he would come over to me
and follow me home. I walked quickly to the corner and then stopped
and looked back. He had not followed me but was still standing in the
same place looking at me. I ran home as fast as I could. I have never seen
him again.

Before I went to college in 1980, my mother told me, "You have
grown up, but I want to remind you not to forget that you once made a
big mistake." I was so angry that I interrupted her for the first time in
my life, saying, "I know what I should remember and what I should forget. I don't need you to remind me!"

During my college life, I refused to talk to any male classmates. I was
afraid that any conversation with them would bring more trouble. One
day the political instructor for my class asked me to come to his office.
He said he wanted to remind me to pay attention to my behavior. He
was told that I had been seen alone in a classroom with a male classmate. I tried to explain that the classmate had asked me for help in

math; I did not volunteer. The political instructor would not let me finish. He interrupted me and said, "That's enough. I just want to remind you for your own sake not to forget your past." It was a punch in the face. My past is a ghost that shadows me. The authorities at my junior high school had placed a bad record in my personal file. It followed me to senior high and then to college.

After graduation, my parents started to introduce boys to me whom they thought fit for my future marriage. I refused them all.

One day my mother asked me, "Tell me the truth. Do you still remember Liu Bin?" I did not know how to respond to this question. How could I forget him? Although we did not even get to shake hands once, he has followed me ever since. The reputation he brought to me cannot be erased. At the same time what my parents did to me cannot be forgiven. Sometimes I regret that I did not stop on that rainy day and talk to him.

IN GORKY'S
FOOTSTEPS

*S*ummer *in Chengdu is like summer in New York City: hot and humid.*
One rarely sees the face of the sun but feels toasted nonetheless. Xiaoyue is an
old friend from my childhood. I was supposed to meet him in a da chaguan
at 2:00.[1] *At 2:30, as I was about to leave and find some cooler place to sit, he*
appeared, wearing a white polo shirt, baggy dress pants, and black sneakers.
As usual, he looked wan and tired.

When he smiles, Xiaoyue's teeth are stained with nicotine. When he gets
excited, his overlarge eyes sparkle. Yellow teeth and big black eyes add to the
contrast with his skin. An old Chinese woman who lives down the street
from us thinks he is a TB carrier. Chinese sages would say that his appear-
ance is the payment for a life of smoking, drinking, and womanizing. The
people in his literature circle say his pale, melancholy face makes him look
like a classical poet. He has the air of a Pushkin, especially when he has his
hair curled. But, he says, he does not want to look like Pushkin, who was
very sentimental. He would rather look like Gorky, who was carefree.

For several years Xiaoyue had lived, without the benefit of marriage, with
a beautiful, celebrated dancer, which created lots of gossip in our neighbor-
hood. Then one day the dancer left him for a doctor. After that he got some-
what more gentle treatment from the neighbors, who claimed that the
dancer had lived with him only so that she could get to his father, a play-
wright who had written a dance drama based on a Tibetan legend for her.

---

1. A *da chaguan* is a teahouse frequented by businessmen.

While waiting for Xiaoyue in the teahouse, I planned to ask him about his personal life, to catch up on things as old friends should. But before I got a chance to ask him about anything, he burst out with, "Boy! On the way here I ran into Aunt Liu. You know, the composer? Right away she starts saying, 'Why are you not married yet? You're pushing forty now. Who is that girl that lives in your house?'"

"Yes," I said, glad to have a chance to ask. "Who is that girl?"

"Her name is Xiaozhao," he said, "and I'm going to get rid of her. She doesn't like my father. Last night my father was making dinner. I was in the living room trying to make a deal with an antique dealer for a Song dynasty teacup. Xiaozhao started shouting at my father. She accused him of putting too much oil in the fish we were having for dinner. He tried to explain that the dish needed that much oil, and she called him a hopeless boor. You know I don't like anyone who abuses my dad.

My relationship with my father has long been strange. I do not know whether I should love him or hate him or both.

My father has a lovely side to his personality. When he wants, he can be honest and sincere—his company at these times is a genuine joy. At other times, however, he is aware of how different and unique he is in comparison to the rest of society. When he shows his conceit, he is unbearable. Consequently, there are times when I love him and other times when I hate him and wish he would die.

One day when I was a teenager and too old for him to control or discipline, I purposely drove him so crazy that he lay in bed wailing, "Woe the day my son was born! I don't want to live anymore. Oh, life is no longer meaningful." I just stood by his bed and laughed at him, while he bemoaned his fate. "Go ahead and really weep if you are so sad," I said. "Don't just sound the thunder without letting it rain. No more acting!"

You should not take this to mean that I don't respect my father. I once told my girlfriend, "When it comes to my father, I have only one. But when it comes to a wife, I can always find a replacement." I expected her to treat him correctly. I was always there for him. I would not allow anyone to be impolite to him. However, my respect for my father should not be thought of as an expression of my love for him either. I more pitied him than loved him. I think the conflicting feelings I had for my father came from my crazy political activities during the Cultural Revolution. It was during those years that I came to understand the ways of the world.

I was one year old in 1958 when my father was pilloried in the Antirightists Campaign of the CCP. The Party and Mao cheated my father, a playwright, just as they cheated thousands of other writers throughout the country. Like many Chinese intellectuals, my father was naive. He believed what Mao had said. He spoke out, suggesting improvements in the way literature could serve the Party. And like most of his naive colleagues, he was quickly branded a counterrevolutionary. However, unlike his colleagues, my father was lucky. He was not sent to the countryside camps to be reformed through labor. He was allowed to remain at his work institution. He was forced to write confessions and stand in front of his coworkers and receive their criticism. My mother, a beautiful actress, did not want her career spoiled, so she divorced my father in 1960. He was granted custody of me because my mother did not want me. I was two years old when she left.

An old Chinese saying says that a family without a woman is like a man without a soul. This certainly fit our existence. My father was kept busy writing his confessions every day. This often meant that there was no food in the house, which was always a mess. As soon as I was big enough, I was forced by circumstances to take over the female role in the house, doing the cooking, washing, and mending of our clothes.

My father did not appreciate my efforts. He frequently beat me if I burned the food or did not clean the dishes thoroughly. One day he came home looking unhappy. He did not sit down to eat dinner, and I did not dare eat all by myself. Very cautiously I begged him to eat a little bit and handed him a bowl of rice with some vegetables. He slapped the bowl out of my hand. It broke on the ground. He ordered me to stand facing the wall. He pulled off my pants and beat me, screaming, "I'll let you eat! Eat, eat. You only know eat." I felt wronged. Although I was crying hard, he did not seem satisfied. Instead he grabbed me by my ankles and hung me over the edge of our fourth-floor balcony. "Stop crying or I'll drop you," he said.

From that moment on I hated him with all my heart. I made a wish in my heart every evening before I went to bed. I wished I would grow full size overnight so I would be able to gain my revenge.

In 1966 when the Cultural Revolution started, my father was serving in the Mass Art Organization of Sichuan. He took the Cultural Revolution as an opportunity for him to regain his standing in the Party. He and a few of his colleagues, most of them younger, launched a newspaper called *Hongwei Bao* [Red Soldiers' Paper] in the summer of 1967. My father was managing editor. The chief editor was a young man.

The paper was 16mo and sold for four fen [about one cent] per issue.[2] Every story in the paper was a diatribe about how so-and-so was a counterrevolutionary working to undermine the Party and was a threat to Mao's revolutionary line. My father sent me into the streets to sell his newspaper.

At the end of each day I turned all my money over to the chief editor. One day I was short four fen. The chief editor pulled off his belt and hit me across the face. He did not ask me about the shortage of four fen before he got his belt. He shouted at me, "You have to pay it back. This is not a money issue. This is a matter of the Revolution." My father was standing there watching, as if I were somebody else's son.

I had an explanation for the shortage of four fen, and I begged the two of them to listen to me. I told them that I had met a worker that afternoon who seemed to like our paper very much. He confessed that he had no money with him to pay for the paper. I thought that the paper needed more proletarian readers and supporters, so I told the man that he could have the paper and not to worry about the money. I would collect from him the next day. I begged their forgiveness for my deed.

---

2. A mo is a measure of paper size. A standard U.S. newspaper is 8mo. A 16mo paper is one-half that size.

Once he heard my story, the chief editor looked pleased and said, "Workers! Very good! You don't need to pay for the shortage."

My father then followed the chief editor. "I know my son is a good boy. He will turn out to be a leader in the Revolution."

I was a bit shocked by their naïveté and the success of my story, which I had just made up on the spot to avoid the beating. In fact, I had spent the four fen on a popsicle because it was hot that day and I was thirsty.

The next day I decided to leave home, partially because I was tired of my father's heavy-handed treatment and partially because I was fascinated by the stories of Maxim Gorky. I had read many of his books where he talked about wandering around the world carefree. And I was crazy about the sea. I had never ever seen the sea. I wrote a poem to my father and walked out the house. The poem read:

> *Dad,*
> *Oh, farewell to those elements*
> *that trouble a free soul.*
> *I am leaving to seek the sea.*
> *I am leaving to wander the world,*
> *to travel in the footsteps of Gorky.*

It was a funny way to start a letter, by quoting Pushkin's poem "To the Sea." It sounded more like homework than a note from a kid about to run away from home.

I did not take any food ration coupons from the house. My understanding of the wandering life was that I was supposed to beg or work for my living. The only thing I took with me were three books: *Long Live the Victory of Mao Zedong's Thought, A Critique of Hegel's Philosophy,* and *Wild Grass,* by Lu Xun.

I had so little knowledge about the world I was about to explore that I thought the sea was to the north of the city where I lived, so I went to the railway station in the northern part of the city. In those days people were allowed to get on the train by showing their platform tickets, so I bought a platform ticket with five fen. There were so many trains in the station, some going south, some going north. I boarded the train for Xi'an, the capital city of Shaanxi Province.

That night I slept underneath a seat in one of the coaches. I was lucky that I did not get caught by the ticket conductors. Late the next day the train arrived at Xi'an. I snuck out of the station, hungry from my trip. I thought I might beg for food in a nearby restaurant, but when I got inside, I decided that begging was too humbling an experience. Realizing that I could not go without food, I promised myself I would think of something else tomorrow. That night I slept in the square outside the railway station. There were hundreds of people there. Most of them were from the countryside, waiting for tickets to take them anyplace they might find opportunities for a better life.

The next morning when I awoke, I remembered Gorky's stories about working in a bakery. However, since all food establishments in China were owned by the government, there was no way for me to go to work in one of them without a permit. I would have to beg or starve.

I walked back into the restaurant, past the table of a kindly looking woman, rehearsing what I was about to say again and again, but I couldn't force my mouth to say the words. The woman stood up and I panicked. "Come on," I thought, "this is your last chance." The woman turned to look at me. Suddenly she reminded me of my mother. I lost my nerve. I was ashamed, as if begging would take away my mother's face. I turned to leave, but the woman stopped me and told me to sit in her place. She walked to the counter and returned with two steamed buns in her hands. She put the buns on the table and said in a soft voice, "Eat and go to school." I remembered hearing the mother of the girl in the next apartment saying the exact same words to her daughter each morning. I was touched by this strange woman. For a moment I thought of her as my mother. I wanted to tell her I was out there to escape the cruelty of my father and to experience the world, but she left before I could say anything. This strange woman's good heart increased my hatred for my father.

After breakfast I went sightseeing. Xi'an is China's ancient capital, and there are a great number of ancient cultural attractions, like the terra-cotta army of the Qin dynasty. I felt free and cheerful as I wandered around in the Dayan Buddhist pagoda.[3] When the wild geese flew back to the nests built up on the top of the pagoda, I realized it was evening. I walked back to the station square to sleep with the other wanderers.

Early in the morning of the next day, I was roused suddenly from my sleep by loud voices. Several men were working their way through the crowd checking the identification cards of the people sleeping in the square. They were all wearing a red armband with two Chinese characters: *Zhi qin* [Be on duty]. None of them were wearing police uniforms, so the armband meant that they were street security guards.

Three men moved toward me. "*Zhengjian!* [identification documents]." What was I supposed to show them? I thought that only government employees had identification cards. I was a student in middle school, but I did not even have a student ID.[4] I told the security guards that I was not a bad person on the run. I was traveling to learn about life, like Gorky. They laughed and called me a liar. They pushed me into a group of other people who had no proper papers. We were taken to the police substation at the railway terminal.

No officer in the police substation ever questioned me further. Three days later, without explanation, I was transferred to the local jail. The following day I was taken to a dairy in Xi'an. A official of the dairy took me to a shop that produced wafers. He said that I would start my reform through labor there. Workers in the shop looked at me as though I were a chicken sent in for their lunch. My dream of wandering the world was over.

By talking to my more friendly looking coworkers, I found out that the prisoners in the dairy were all untried criminals. Some were thieves, and some were traders in human beings. Most were peasants. Many had abducted children or women and then sold them in other cities. I

---

3. The Greater Wild Goose Pagoda is known for the wild geese that nest in its eaves.
4. In China a person has to have a certificate from the local authorities to travel.

couldn't believe that I had been caged with such people or that my "crime" was a bad as theirs.

At the jail every morning, we prisoners ran four circles around the courtyard of the jail. Then we were allowed to wash our faces and brush our teeth in a large tub that looked like a horse-watering trough. In the evening we cleaned our feet in the same tub. The water was changed only once every three or four days. Then we recited Mao's quotations in the courtyard. We were fed one bowl of porridge twice a day. We were always hungry.

At the end of every day as we returned from the factory, we walked past a big bowl full of smashed wafers, set out to feed a large ferocious guard dog. Every day we swarmed the bowl like bees, fighting over the dog's food. I never got to it even once because I was the shortest and the weakest among the group.

I began to miss my father and decided that I did not want to go on any more adventures. I did forced labor in the dairy for three months. Then I was sent back to the holding camp at the railway station in Xi'an. From there I would be sent back home. I wrote a letter to my father: "Dad, I will be home in one week. Please meet me at the Municipal Collection Post."

People in the Xi'an holding camp were not allowed outside the camp except for those doing forced labor in nearby factories. A young man who was one of the laborers agreed to mail my letter for me. I promised him I would help him in the future anytime he needed because I would free soon.

A few days later, with a dozen others I was sent to Rongcheng. Like everyone else, the jailers at the Municipal Collection Post shaved my head, just like the jailers in Xi'an had done.

The most humiliating thing about life, however, was eating. After my head was shaved, I was given a bamboo stick about the size of my index finger. The stick was marked with a ideograph that I didn't recognize. I thought it was an evil sign. I asked an older prisoner, one who had been in the post for more than a year, what the character meant. He told me that it meant *jisheng chong* [parasite]. It stood for the idea that we were eating the rice of the country, but we did not make contributions to the general welfare. We were parasites. This made me angry, but there was nothing I could do about the humiliation I felt. At mealtime, we exchanged the stick for a bowl of rice with a little preserved vegetable. After eating, we washed the rice bowl and returned it to another counter and then got our stick back. If we lost our sticks, we didn't eat.

On the fourth afternoon I was there, I heard my full name called by an officer of the post. I followed him to the admissions office. There was my father. Just as I was about to call to him, my father stood up and greeted the officer. He acted as if he did not see me at all. He told the officer, "Hrmph. This kid wanted to learn from Gorky. He just did himself harm. He deserved the reform through labor." As he said this, he was smiling. I didn't understand what was going on until the officer told me that I could leave with my father. He sent me to gather my things from the dormitory.

Before I was allowed to leave the post, however, the officer checked my body and my small schoolbag. He confiscated my diary, poems, and the sketches I drew for the other prisoners. Reading one of the poems, the officer asked, "You are criticizing the Revolution, aren't you?" When I denied his accusations, he said, "Listen to this: So high is the gray wall, so free the little birds outside the wall."

His reading embarrassed me because those words were my thoughts, my real feelings, not a real poem.

He asked me, "What's the implication here, heh?"

"I did not write it," I said, lying. "I copied that line from a collection of poetry written by revolutionary martyrs."

The officer was confused and frustrated by what I said. I knew he thought I was lying but wasn't sure. He remained silent for a few seconds and then said, "You are not allowed to take any written items when you leave. You can go now."

The moment we were out of sight of the jail, my father began to berate me for running off. "You are definitely wrong. You never take my advice. If I were an officer in that jail, I wouldn't have released you."

I was shocked. Imagine. For more than three months, I had not had enough to eat. I was weak and starving. Now my father was criticizing me like the officers in the jail rather than being concerned about my welfare. My feeling of missing him slipped out of my soul, and the idea of wandering again captured me.

Leaving home would have to wait, however. I was too insulted to appear in public, especially in the light of day, because of my shaved head. Shaved heads were the symbol of criminals and hooligans. I asked my father if we could go home first. I needed a bath. He took me home and gave me a little money before he left for work.

I went to a public bathhouse and took a bath. I still had some money left, which would afford me a cup of tea. But it was still bright at six o'clock in the afternoon. I decided to wait until dark before going to the teahouse.

Given my luck, I shouldn't have gone to the teahouse. It was there that I ran into an old neighbor, Chen Hong, and two of his friends. Chen and I were never friends; I only knew him because we lived in the same housing complex and his father was a writer, too. I supposed that Chen must have known where I had been for the past three months. He came over to my tea table and tapped my shoulder. "What are you doing here? You look pale. Let us take you out for dinner." I took his invitation, so I didn't have to listen to my father's accusations over the meal at home.

On the way to a local restaurant near my home, Chen showed me a Tibetan knife. He knew I liked to collect knives and wanted to show off his new acquisition. I took a good, long look at his new piece. I was excited by its elegance and delicacy.

Before we went into the restaurant, I wanted to smoke. I borrowed some money from Chen, and I stepped across the street into a tobacco shop. While waiting to pay for my cigarettes, I heard screaming outside. "Murder! Murder!" I dashed into the street to see people rushing toward the restaurant where we had planned to go.

I looked across the street. Chen's two friends had disappeared. Chen stood outside the door to the restaurant waving a dagger at one of the employees. His opponent had pulled a pair of fire tongs out of a stove. The tongs were red with heat. He tried to stab Chen with the tongs. I realized that the situation was far from good and made off immediately.

I was out of breath when I got home. My father immediately said, "So you made a blunder again. You looked scared. So what was it this time?" I told him what I had seen and that I was worried about Chen. My father did not seem to believe me. I went to Chen's father's house to see whether Chen was home. He was not. I had a hunch that was a bad sign. Just after I finished my dinner, two policemen came to the door. They did not show me an arrest warrant. They only said, "Come with us," and then they handcuffed me.

At the police department, I told the policemen how I met Chen at the teahouse and how we went to the restaurant and how I left him to go buy some cigarettes. I told them all the details. One of the policemen shouted at me, "None of your tricks! You must come clean! Chen has confessed his crime already."

Yujia zhezhui, hehuan wuci [He who has a mind to beat his dog will easily find a stick]. I was sent to the city prison, charged with attempted murder and robbery. No lawyer, no court hearing, no justice. The police department allowed my father to bring me a quilt, toothbrush, soap, and some clothes. I was not allowed to see him. I was totally wrecked both physically and spiritually. My "crime" would mean at least five years in prison. I thought I was finished.

One day a large number of inmates were sent to the subdistrict office where we came from. We were told that we would be paraded through the streets, exposed in public as criminals.

Before the parade there was to be a *douzheng hui* [struggle meeting] where we would be stood up in front of an audience of our previous neighbors in a local meeting hall and criticized for our crimes against the state. The whole neighborhood would be there because the *douzheng hui* was advertised on bulletin boards around the community.

We were not given breakfast in the jail that day. The humiliation parade was to take place in the afternoon. I felt like I would starve. While waiting for my humiliation, I saw a daughter of my downstairs neighbor, Zhong Lin. She was working in the subdistrict office. I asked her to inform my father of my plight and to bring me some food. She agreed to tell him when she went home for lunch.

My father did not come. I was dizzy and weak because of starvation and my father's absence. At that moment I would have been willing to be executed.

At three o'clock in the afternoon, an officer of the jail tied my hands together by my thumbs and shoved them up behind my back. Around my neck he hung a huge board that said, "Attempted murderer and robber Xiaoyue." My name had been crossed through with a large splash of red ink. I was pushed into a truck to stand in front of two armed policemen.

The parade of trucks started. I was paraded past my home. I had hoped that my father would be in the crowd outside the housing complex gate. His presence would mean a lot to me. At least it would show he still cared for me. I searched the crowd and was disappointed again. My father was not there.

The trucks traveled through the city commercial centers and then carried me to my old middle school. At the school the prison officials held another *douzheng hui* so all the students would recognize me as an evil person. An officer of the jail announced my "crimes" and then urged the students to be aware of bad influences from society. He said that they should all study hard for the Revolution and become Red Successors of Socialism.

After the Struggle Meeting, an ironic and touching thing occurred. A few minutes after I had been taken back to the subdistrict office, a young boy was brought in front of me by an officer. The officer said, "Behave yourself or else." The boy nodded constantly, "Yes! Yes!" When the officer left the room, the boy said, "Here. You must be hungry." He took a mess tin out of his schoolbag and said, "It's not a great meal but better than nothing, right? Hurry and eat before it gets cold."

I was more stunned than moved for a few seconds. I did not know this boy at all. Usually people would not risk their well-being to help or pity a bad person, especially someone who had been branded a criminal. I reminded him, "Didn't you watch the parade of criminals this afternoon? Do you know I am one of them? Why do you bring me a meal?"

"Because we were schoolmates," he answered, "except I was one year behind you. I was at the *douzheng hui* at school, but I had a feeling you were not as bad a person as they said. I overheard someone say that you hadn't eaten anything the whole day. So I told the officer I was a relative of yours."

He left without telling me his name. I was so moved that I couldn't swallow the meal. The young boy's behavior added to my hatred for my father—blood was not thicker than water after all. I promised myself that if I ever got out of jail, I would never acknowledge my father again.

About a year later at lunch one day, the server in the prison cafeteria offered me a second helping of a special preserved vegetable. This was unusual. My heart sank. I figured I had finally been sentenced to be executed. Right after lunch a warden called me from my cell and took me to the office of the jail director.

The director asked me, "Where are your belongings?"

"In my cell," I answered, feeling scared.

The director called another prisoner to fetch my belongings. Then he said to me, "We have informed your father of your release. Go to the gate to see if he's here yet."

This was strange. When I was arrested and put into jail, I was asked to sign many documents relating to my "crime." When I was released, I was not given any explanation whatsoever. I was not provided with any papers to sign to say I was clear or the case was dismissed. Even today I have no idea what the officers of the jail wrote in my records.

When the prisoner returned with my belongings, I was taken through the courtyard to the main gate of the jail. At the gate the warden said, "Wait here for your father." He opened the gate and I walked out of the prison. I was totally lost. I looked around but still didn't understand that I was free until I heard the gate clang closed behind me. Yes, I was free, but where was my father? I could not believe he was not there again. I headed home immediately to pick a fight with my father. I accused him of being completely selfish, concerned only with his own reputation.

"Since you have no faith in me, why don't you go ahead and declare in the newspaper that we have ended our father-and-son relationship?" I asked him.

"I don't think the police department made a mistake when they took you to jail. You have totally destroyed my face," he replied.

I might have understood if someone else had said this to me, but he was not somebody else. Although he was my father, he only wanted to act like everyone else. No one would give me a chance to defend myself, to clarify the facts, to rehabilitate my reputation.

For a long time I liked to think my cup of sadness was full. I hoped this cup could pass from me sooner. I don't think this way anymore. All my experience tells me that I was luckier than a lot of people. Not everyone could have a father like mine, so frustrating, so selfish, and so blindly loyal to the Party. My life with my father made me an experienced and mature man. All this does not mean I have forgiven my father. I still can't help wishing he were dead.

CLASS ORIGINS

One afternoon I was sitting in my hotel room in Beijing, sorting out my materials for this book, when there was a knock at my door. I opened the door and got a wonderful surprise. Standing there was an old friend, Zhoujing, and a small boy.

Zhoujing is an agricultural researcher and reporter. In the past he and I had worked together on stories for Xinhua. He had run into a mutual friend in Beijing who said I was in town and was writing a book.

Unlike the people in the States, Chinese people are not generally conscious of the symbolic meaning of clothing. They will wear whatever comes to hand, not changing for an interview, especially when the interviewer is an old friend. So I was not surprised when Zhoujing appeared in my room in a rayon pin-striped shirt, coffee brown polyester slacks, and a pair of black imitation leather sandals. His sleeves were rolled up, and I could see where the cuffs were stained with sweat. He did not wear an undershirt. His trousers were as wrinkled as lettuce leaves. His small eyes were puffy from lack of sleep, making them look even smaller. I could not believe that the man standing in front of me was the senior editor of a major newspaper in Beijing.

I teased him. "You look like a peasant."

"But my son doesn't," he replied proudly.

His son was neatly dressed in a shirt with small flowers and black pants. Obviously the old saying "Like father, like son" did not apply.

"Oh," I said, "your son is very handsome. You must have a pretty wife."

"Yes, he's my son. And very naughty, too," he answered, as the boy began bouncing up and down on the bed.

"You spoil him," I replied, not trying to hide my disapproval. "That's not good."

"Yes. But I don't see anything wrong with that. I want him to grow up totally unlike me. I want his body free, his heart free, and his thinking free. I don't want him to live like I did as a child."

As he began talking, the boy began singing and dancing to the music from the television. As Zhoujing told me his story, his eyes followed the boy around the room.

Have you ever gone through the experience of falling from a model student to an outcast just because of your father's past? Well, I did.

I was the best student in all of my classes, the teacher's pet, if you like. Before the Cultural Revolution, whenever school activities called for a representative, I was always the first candidate chosen and always won a place on the team.

One afternoon in the summer of 1967, the authorities at my school called an urgent meeting. The principal said that ten students would be elected to participate in an interview that Chairman Mao would grant to young people at Tiananmen in Beijing.

Sitting in the classroom, I was confident that I would be elected. The election was done by secret ballot. When the votes were all cast, a pretty girl whose seat was in front of mine was called to the front of the room to call out the votes. She read the list of names and the vote totals in order from most votes received to the least. The first name called was a classmate's who was just an average student. Strange. Then another one who was constantly being sent to the principal for causing problems in the classroom. The roll went on and on. Finally my name was called, but I got only two votes. At that point my ears were ringing, my face was hot, and my eyes were filled with tears. It was the biggest insult I had ever received.

When the last person's name was called and the last ballot counted, I was out of the game. I dashed out of the classroom, trying to leave the looks from my classmates behind me. They seemed to be saying that everyone knew why I had lost so badly. I ran to the principal's office and knocked on the door, demanding an explanation.

The principal was icy cold. "Young man, go home and think about your class origins."

What about my class origins? My grandfather had been a successful jeweler but lost all his money before he died. In order to make a living, my father left home at the age of thirteen and went to Shanghai to work in a food cannery. Two years later Shanghai was liberated by the communists. The food company was nationalized by the government. His job lost, my father came back to his hometown and married my mother, the daughter of a local landowner, the following year. Now he was an accountant at the local candy factory. What could be wrong with that?

Class origins. Class origins. The term buzzed in my head all the way home. Ever since elementary school, whenever I had to fill in any form I always put "worker" in the blank under "family background." I belonged to the working class. I knew that I should have been included in the revolutionary team.

At the entrance to the street to my house, I bumped into a neighbor. She asked me the embarrassing question, "When are you going to Beijing?"

I told her, "I won't be going to Beijing." Her smile disappeared as I walked into our courtyard.

My mother was waiting for me with more heartbreaking news. The boy living next door to us was going to Beijing on the interview team from another school. This was very strange. He was known around the neighborhood as a troublemaker who never did well in school. I was just the opposite, the pride of our street because of my hard work and good grades.

I wanted to cry, but instead I shouted, "It's unfair. What is my father? Is he a member of the working class or not?"

My mother looked confused and scared. "Your father was accused of being a capitalist this morning. The factory managers broadcast, 'Down with the capitalist dog Zhou Jingtang over the public address system.' Do you think it's fair for your father?" This was the first time I remember hearing my mother raise her voice.

That evening my father came home later than usual. His clothes were dirty and his face was scratched. He had been roughed up by Rebels at the factory and then criticized for an hour before they would let him leave. I was so selfish at the time that I did not try to comfort him.

Instead I confronted him. "You are a liar. You told me that you and your boss were standing on the sidewalk waving a red flag to welcome the People's Liberation Army when they liberated Shanghai. You said you supported the Communist Party, but you are just a hidden capitalist."

My father was as much hurt as shocked by my claims. Fighting back his tears, he said, "You are too young to understand. I am not a capitalist."

I should have been on my father's side, but I could not act rationally. During that crazy period of the Cultural Revolution, not many people could, and I was no exception. All I knew was that I was in trouble and it wasn't because of anything I had done. Because of my "capitalist" father, I dropped to the bottom of society. I was no longer allowed to participate in any social activities. We lived in a small coastal town where everyone knew everyone else. They also knew everyone's class origins. There was no privacy, and there was no escape. People's personal feelings and attitudes toward me changed as soon as my father was accused. Where before they had pointed to me as an exemplary student, telling their children to imitate me, now they used me as an example when it came to disciplining their children.

All the children refused to play with me. When they saw me in the street, they would spit on me and sing:

> Dog, dog, capitalist dog.
> The father is a big dog.
> The son is a little one.

I spent most of those days wishing someone in the Party would re-
classify my father as a proletarian or a peasant. Anything would be better than being labeled a capitalist.

One deep autumn morning in 1969, two men came to my house.
One was as weathered as dried weeds. He wore a peasant's straw hat.
His clothes were made of home-woven cloth and barely covered his
bony body. His feet were bare. The younger man looked like he suffered
from Down's syndrome. My father bowed to the older man when he let
them in. They sat in the living room talking in low voices.

At noon my father insisted they have lunch with us. My mother
made special food for them. At the table they stayed silent. My father
constantly added food to their bowls. After lunch my father walked
with them as they left. I saw him insist that they take some money. He
gave them two yuan [about 40 cents]. The older man had tears running
down his face.

My father looked sad as he came back into the house. I asked him
who the men were. He said the older man was his old boss, the owner of
the food company where he worked in Shanghai.

I got angry. I began berating him like one of the Rebels, criticizing
him, "Don't you have any sense of class borders? That man was a capitalist. He exploited you. Why are you still sympathetic with him?"

"You understand nothing," my father replied. "How could he exploit
me? He was not a law-breaking capitalist. He established that food
company through thrift and hard work. He was my savior. Without his
help I would have been dead years ago. When the Party confiscated his
company, they also took his life. They hounded and persecuted his entire family. He has gone through much much more than you could ever
imagine. His wife committed suicide. That young man is his son, his
only child." At this point my father burst out crying.

I was not touched or convinced by my father's story. The next day I
did something horrible: I went to the Party committee at the candy factory and told them my father had problems coping with the Revolution. Not only was he sympathetic with capitalists, but he had also
treated his capitalist former boss to lunch. That afternoon the Rebels

came and took my father away. My father suffered heavy physical and emotional abuse in their custody. As a result, he was left partially paralyzed.

The treatment I received from my neighbors because of my class origins struck terror in me. As a consequence, I would do anything to get reclassified. Turning my father over to the revolutionary Rebels was only the start. The authorities at my school told me I needed to make painstaking efforts if I really wanted to be accepted by the working class.

The next one to suffer was my mother. As I mentioned, she was from a well-to-do family. Her actions jeopardized not only my life but also our family because my mother was a pious Buddhist and kept an altar in our living room.

In those days almost every family in the country had some kind of shrine or picture of Mao in the house. In our house we had a statue of Mao, sitting on a small covered stand under a glass case. Under the stand for Mao was my mother's statue of the Buddha. Every morning and night when she bowed to Mao, she was actually praying to the Buddha behind him. In front of the statue was a bronze incense burner that had belonged to my mother's ancestors.

Every time my mother lit her incense, she was worshiping Buddha. In those days only one belief was legitimate—belief in Mao and the Party. I was afraid that my mother's incense burner would bring chaos to our family rather than the peace and safety my mother prayed for.

One day the Rebels raided two households in our neighborhood. Later I heard a rumor that my family was next on their list. I waited until my mother took my father to a local Chinese medical practitioner, and I hammered the incense burner into pieces. But destroying the burner did not relieve me of my terror.

I did not dare throw the pieces in the dump because someone might find them. I had to hide them because I knew the burner was meaningful to my mother.

I wrapped the pieces in newspaper and hid them under Mao's statue and replaced the burner with a plain ceramic bowl filled with sand.

Then for the first time, I burned incense in front of Mao's statue. Strangely, I felt the existence of Buddha at that moment. I spent the rest of the morning trying to think up a story to tell my mother when she asked what happened to the burner.

Fortunately for me, she didn't ask me about the burner. Instead, when she discovered that it was missing, she said, "I guess our family's ancient incense burner must be out having fun. It probably got lost somewhere." Her sense of humor surprised me and made me feel guilty. I did not say a word.

She looked at me without speaking for several minutes and then said, "You are too young to understand. The Buddha is not a demon or deity. He is as real as Chairman Mao." She burned incense in front of Mao's statue that night as usual.

For me, however, my mother's understanding was more painful than her yelling at me or beating me. The broken burner appeared in my dreams again and again. Worried that my mother would find my secret under the statue when she cleaned up the house, I took it and hid it underneath my mattress.

A few weeks later a tinker came though our village hawking repaired woks and looking for work. My mother sent me out to get an enamel basin repaired. There were a few women around the tinker. I heard him ask the women if they had any "Olds" they would like altered into something else. He said that he used to be a jewelry craftsman but that the Cultural Revolution had forced him to shift his career to repair work.

An idea crossed my mind. Waiting until everyone had left, I asked the repairer, "Can you turn bronze into something useful?"

"Young man, I even can turn a stone into a beautiful ornament. Why? Have you stolen your grandmother's statue of the Buddha?"

"Not really," I said. "You will see."

I ran home and returned with the wrapped pieces of the broken burner. I asked him to turn the pieces into a serving spoon. He returned the next day with two spoons.

That night I asked my mother to cook soup for dinner. When the soup was presented at the dinner table, I thrust the spoons into the soup bowl. The soup bowl was large and held a lot of soup, and the spoons could not stand up in the bowl. They sank quickly to the bottom of the bowl. My mother pulled them out with a pair of chopsticks. I was expecting a smile when she saw the spoons, but instead she asked, "Where did these spoons come from? We don't have bronze spoons."

"I traded our old incense burner for them," I replied. I thought she would be pleased because the spoons were pretty. She didn't say anything. She cleaned the spoons, dried them, and put them away. I have not seen them since that day.

It has been twenty years since that day. I travel a lot in my job, and everywhere I go in China, north and south, I look for an incense burner for my mother. But I have never found one. I know I won't find one. Nothing can replace my lost heritage.

PRESUMED GUILT

Lingmu is the chief economics editor of a major magazine in Beijing. During our interview, I could see the division in Lingmu's life. His eyes, behind black-framed glasses perched on the end of his nose, showed wisdom and honesty but also a heavy heart. Part of his life is devoted to his research, writing, and editing. The other part is consumed with endless office politics. The lack of alternatives to playing these games has left deep tracks across his forehead and spider webs of lines radiating from the corners of his eyes to his temples. He is thirty-five years old.

Lingmu likes to talk about Freud, especially his Interpretation of Dreams.

"Our generation used to live for others, for our parents, for our country, worst of all, for the opinions of others. We always worried about how others would respond to our words and deeds. For us, the collective consciousness was supreme, and individuality was reduced almost to zero. But how can you reduce your subconscious? For a long time I felt like all my dreams were planned. They were just a summary of what took place during the day. Now I rarely dream of anything. What a difference it makes. Life is a dream that cannot be interpreted."

I would like to tell you a little bit about my father's family background before I start my story. My father is the youngest of five children. His father was a general engineer for the Long-Hai railway.[1]

---

1. This railway runs from Liangyun Harbor in Jiangsu Province to Lanzhou, the capitol of Gansu Province. Construction was started in 1905 and covers 1,759 km. The railway is the main artery of transportation linking the western and the eastern parts of China.

In his capacity as a railway engineer, my grandfather traveled a lot, widening his horizons about the world and opening his heart to new thoughts, both technical and political ones. Thanks to this open-minded father, my father and his sisters and brothers were devoted to the communist revolution.

My father became a Party member in Yan'an when he was only fourteen. He was thrown into jail twice by the KMT. The first time occurred when he was seventeen. This event turned out to be beneficial. One of his cellmates had mastered three foreign languages—French, German, and English. He taught my father English.

The KMT's prison system encouraged study. Prisoners were allowed to study anything: literature, philosophy, the hard sciences, whatever they liked. Prisoners were even allowed to take the entrance exam for the university. My father must have had gifts for language and social sciences. In prison he had no access to reading materials in English, but by studying an English dictionary and talking with his cellmate, he mastered enough of the language that he was able to pass the 1942 entrance exam for the universities. He was accepted by the Foreign Language Department of Northwest University (today's Qinghua University). He came in first place among thousands of examinees in the northern part of the country.

My father was denied permission to enter the university unless he first renounced his membership in the Chinese Communist Party. He refused. After some negotiating with the local KMT commander, he was allowed to attend the university on the condition that he not engage in any political activities. The commander promised my father that he would not disclose this agreement to anyone. My father was so naive that he believed the commander would live up to his promise. He also thought that he would be able to contribute more to the Party and the communist cause if he could get out of jail without betraying his political comrades. He signed the agreement. The KMT published it in the newspapers.

My father's second arrest took place when he graduated from the university in 1948. He was accused of starting a student movement against the KMT. He was bailed out of jail by the daughter of Fu Zuoyi, the mayor of Beijing, just before the 1949 Revolution reached the city limits.

At the end of 1949, the Party made my father editor in chief of a major newspaper in Beijing. Ironically, he was put in a powerful position even though he was not a Party member. The local cadres told him that his membership status was under investigation because of his activities before liberation. In other words, the Party did not trust him.

The membership issue was a cross my father carried his whole life. The Party is sometimes fond of talking about human rights because it would like to think of itself as the most humane ruling party. However, the Party never really says what it means by human rights. The freedom to think, the freedom to participate in social movements, and the freedom to speak are my definition of human rights. The Party also talks about liberating people. Liberty is another vague concept. Political action cannot be called liberating unless an individual as a human being feels free. It is this sense of freedom that marks the reality of human rights.

For my father, the clearing of his reputation from before the Revolution and membership in the Party would be his liberation. However, Party membership is like bait. It seems to be reachable sometimes if you can make the jump. But the Party moves the brass ring higher and higher, just out of reach, whenever you try.

The Cultural Revolution was the perfect chance for the Party to totally take away my father's hope. I will never forget that summer afternoon in 1967. Even now, as I am talking to you, I can still feel the humidity and heat of that day.

I was home from school. My family lived in some apartments that belonged to the newspaper. The building sat behind the compound of the paper itself. In order to get home, I had to walk through the compound. That afternoon, when I passed the news building, I was shocked by a big-character poster hung on the building. The slogan read, "Dig Out Longtime-Hidden Traitor *XX*." The poster had been written in large black characters, and Father's name had been crossed through with a splash of red ink.

The slogan seemed like a kick in the knees. I was shaking. I dared not turn around. I felt people's eyes behind every window in the building. Eyes above a bad smile, staring at me. I tried to run, but my knees were cold and uncooperative. Unable to move, my mother's voice reached me, "What are you doing here?" Suddenly I realized that I was standing still. My mother looked pale. She took my arm and dragged me home.

Although I was only eight years old, the idea of a traitor was deeply ingrained in my brain from reading and watching movies. Traitors were bad. They all wound up being killed by one or two heroic Party members. I feared my father would die that way.

As we walked home, I cautiously asked my mother, "Is Dad a bad guy? Why did they call him traitor?"

Mom did not answer me, saying instead, "Don't ask. It has nothing to do with you." Then I heard her murmuring, "Ridiculous, it should be clear."

Dad did not come home that night. His mother was living with us. She was the most sensitive old woman I have ever known. Grandma usually went to bed around nine o'clock. Around eleven o'clock she was still awake, so my mother tried to get her to go to bed,

"Go to bed, Mother. Father has an important meeting tonight. He might not be able to be home til morning. Please go to bed."

"Important meeting? Nothing could be as important as Chairman Mao's needs, and even Mao needs to go home and sleep. I'll wait for my son," Grandma spoke without looking up.

Mom released a deep sigh. Then all of a sudden she took after me. "Why are you still here? You have to go to school tomorrow. Go to bed now."

"I don't want to go, " I mumbled, somewhat in fear and somewhat in guilt.

"What?" Mom shouted. "You want to skip school?"

"No!" I screamed. "All my schoolmates will know that Dad is a traitor and that I am the son of a traitor."

"What has happened to my son?" Grandma jumped up. "Why is he not home?"

"Who told you that rubbish?" Mom was getting frustrated. "Remember what Dad taught you? Believe in what you believe in, regardless of what others say. Be a big boy and go to bed now."

Strangely I did feel like an adult then, but I climbed into the twin bed where my four-year-old brother was sound asleep. The whole night I was half awake and half asleep. I could hear Mom and Grandma whispering secrets to each other for a long time.

The next day at school I was beaten up by some older boys. I never heard the reason they beat me, but I did know it had something to do with the big change in my dad's identity from editor in chief to traitor. Once in a while today I can still hear those kids cursing me, "Beat the son of the traitor," while they were kicking me and punching me in the face. I felt ashamed of myself as I ran from them. I wondered if I would turn into a traitor someday because I was a coward, afraid to fight.

When I got home I saw Dad sitting in his chair reading a newspaper. I was so happy that I naively thought he was all right. That made me all right, too. Poof, just like that. All the feelings of shame were gone. All of a sudden I was crying, showing my bloody nose and bruised face, expecting his sympathy and comforting words.

Dad did not give me a hug or comfort me as he usually did when I felt wronged. He did not even glance at me. Not a sound. After a few seconds, he said, "Beat or beaten black and blue. Don't you ever come home again crying."

I could not tell what my Dad's facial expression was. He buried himself behind his newspaper. By his tone, however, I could tell he was upset. But I didn't know with whom—me or the boys who beat me or the Party. I blamed him for not being on my side. When I look back now, I suppose it was his way of giving me an education in how to be a man.

For a long period of time I was uncomfortable with my father. I suffered a great deal because he was labeled a traitor. It created a huge shadow, which would hang over me for the rest of my life.

I was not sad that day in the winter of 1967 when Dad and Mom were pushed into a big truck along with other denounced capitalist roaders. They were being shipped out of Beijing to a poor rural area far from the city. To me, they were like the Russian traitors during the revolution sent into exile in Siberia. I was full of hate and gave a vengeful look to Mom when she waved good-bye to me. Dad's eyes were full of disappointment. I left before the truck.

Soon after my parents were sent away, most of the newspaper's other writers were also sent to the countryside, leaving their children behind. A few of the paper's executives remained in Beijing, assigned to take care of the children left behind. All of us children were organized into study groups. Day after day we studied Chairman Mao's teachings, rehearsed a revolutionary performance, and held meetings for self-criticism.

In my studying group, there was boy named Sun. He was sturdy and tall. His most striking feature was an upturned nose, which caused him to be teased. We claimed his nose could easily catch the rainfall. Before the Cultural Revolution, he was never popular. After our parents were sent away, his remained behind because they were workers and therefore leaders. From that day on, Sun acted as though he was superior to those of us whose parents had been denounced by the Party.

One day the other kids began to say that a popular girl, Xiaoli, liked me. Sun became angry when he learned that the girl was attracted to me and not to him.

In those days the way for a boy to impress a girl was to do something unique, drawing the girl's attention. Sometimes these things were more stupid than unique. One afternoon Sun insisted we arm wrestle. I did not realize his motivation until it was too late. I beat him in front of all the other kids.

From that day on Sun regarded me as his rival in everything. Whatever I did, he always tried to surpass me. In those days I was a pretty fair harmonica player. I practiced every day. One day the adult in charge of our study class told us that there would be a music competition. The best performers would be sent to entertain our parents in the country-side. This was my best chance to visit my mom and dad.

Sun bought a harmonica and began to practice the same musical pieces I played. I wasn't worried as he was far behind me, and I easily beat him in the competition. The day before the delegation was to leave, I was told I would not be going. Sun took my place. I asked the adult for an explanation. He told me that Sun's parents were politically reliable and clear. Later I learned that Sun's mother told the person in charge of the delegation that I should not be allowed to go, regardless of my performing skills, because my father was a traitor.

The harmonica or arm wrestling might not sound like a big deal, but they were the seeds that yielded an evil tree that overshadowed my life.

A week after the kids came back from the parents, I was studying with a large group of kids. Sun suddenly shouted at me, "Lingmu, play-ing on the stage is very satisfying. Do you want to be on the stage? You need to practice more." I noticed that he winked at Xiaoli, a smile hang-ing on the corner of his mouth. I wanted to punch him in the nose, but I did not. I don't know why.

A few days later the military came to our area to recruit new soldiers. Being a soldier was the thing in those days. It looked like the best future for kids in our generation, especially since all the universities were closed down. One kid, Lin Jian, signed up for the army. He passed the first test. His parents were not in political trouble like mine, so he had a clear political pedigree. Lin Jian was worried he might fail the physical exam because he was nearsighted. He was a good friend of mine and asked me to take the physical for him. I agreed.

Our secret leaked out inside the kids' group even before I went to the recruiting station for Lin Jian. After learning of our plan, Sun went to Lin Jian and persuaded him that I would fail because I was too skinny and not tall enough. Slapping his breast, Sun told Lin, "You see how strong I am. I could pass the physical exam and make your dream come true."

Sun went the recruiting station with great confidence, accompanied by me and Lin Jian. Five minutes after he went in, Sun walked out of the examining room with a long face. He had failed the first test. The nurse said he had high blood pressure. He refused to believe it. He hurried to a bigger hospital and another check. The result was the same.

This was a big blow to Sun. He went to the hospital every other day for the next two weeks. Every time the result of the blood pressure check turned out the same.

Sun's mother came to me one day. In a scary voice she said, "My son is ill. It is all your fault. You should not have tried to compete with him. Just whom do you think you are? The son of traitor. It is your responsibility to bring the other children to see my son and tell him he is all right. I will expect you all tonight."

I was scared to death. I went to Sun's house with some other kids that night, but Sun locked himself in his room. He would let only me in. Before I said anything, Sun blurted out, "I am definitely whole. I don't need a physician to prove that. These doctors are just lying to put me down."

I did not know how to respond. He paused for a second, then he asked me, "Do you think we are good friends?"

"Certainly," I answered.

"Then you have to humor me about everything from now on. Your father has some serious political problems, right?"

I was immediately full of hate for Sun, for his parents, and for my father. I wanted to smash Sun like an ant, but I found myself saying, "Yes, yes. You are right." What else I could say besides "yes." Sick or not, he held all the power, and he knew it.

Walking out of Sun's house I really hated Sun, but I heard myself saying, "Dad, why did you do this to me? Now I will never visit you."

Swearing was one thing. Keeping my promise was another. I could not help thinking about my parents, especially when I was lying in bed without anyone to talk to. There was no one in the house except my little brother, now six years old. My grandma had been sent to my uncle's house right before Dad and Mom were sent away from Beijing. Brother was so little. I was the man of a poor house.

My fate was not as bad as the fate of some other people. Instead of being sent to the countryside, as so many thousands of other children were, I was given a job at a local paint factory. Out of fifty new employees I was singled out to be a porter, even though I was the smallest one of the group. My position as a porter was the most humble one in the factory. It was also the most physically demanding. I had to load and unload barrels of dye from trucks. Some barrels weighed as much as 100 kilos.

Why me? My father was alleged a traitor, and one of the security guards of the factory happened to have a wife working as a janitor at the newspaper. The guard knew everything about my father, so he told the paint factory leaders. Soon everyone he knew in the factory knew that I was the son of a traitor and therefore deserved nothing. As far as the managers of the factory were concerned, letting me work as a porter was a huge favor.

I was the son of my father, the son of intelligent parents. Every day after work the other workers played poker to kill the time. I did not hold anything against them, but it was not my kind of entertainment. I needed something different to divert my attention, so I began to study English. I started by reading signs, such as "Flammable Liquid" and "Poison: Do Not Induce Vomiting," on those imported petroleum barrels.

The loading and unloading teams were at the bottom of the social ladder but at the top in terms of cultural quality. Five of us who worked on the team were sons of intellectuals. One was the son of a "historical counterrevolutionary," one was the son of a former KMT official, one was the son of a "political criminal," and I was the son of a "traitor." We used to wonder aloud about how the past of a father could reappear in the present of a son.

There was also a senior engineer on the team. He was with us because he had been denounced by the Party as a counterrevolutionary. He had been educated at Saint John's University in Shanghai before the 1949

Revolution. Most of the teachers at the university had been Western missionaries, and he could speak and write three foreign languages, one of which was English. He was so kind that he spent his free time helping me with my English.

Studying English in this way constantly reminded me of Dad's experiences in prison. The engineer would assign homework for me occasionally. Every time I sat down with my homework, there was a longing to visit Dad. The more English exercises I did, the stronger the longing became.

Economically speaking, it would not be easy to afford such a visit. My monthly salary was forty yuan. Because I was doing physical labor, I got a little more money than the average worker. Even so, it was still difficult to make the fare. A one-way ticket cost about half my monthly salary. Besides my own expenses, I had to support my little brother's education in middle school. My parents had no salary, and they just barely got by. They were given only a small amount of money for living expenses.

By watching my money carefully, I was able to make my first visit to Dad and Mom in the winter of 1973. I packed my English exercises and a jar of fermented bean curd in my school tote, not because it was something special but because it was the only food I could afford after I paid the railway fare.

It took me two nights and one day to get to the rural area where my father and mother were living, if you could call it living. They were assigned to raise pigs, and the room where they lived was not as good as the pigsty. Judging from their living conditions, I sensed their food could not be much better. I was glad I bought them the fermented bean curd.

When I walked into their room, I said, "Dad, I bought you fermented bean curd."

"Did you open it already?" Dad asked strangely.

"No. Why?"

"Well, the whole house smells like bean curd."

I opened my tote and found that the jar was broken. All my English exercises were soaked. I was too disappointed to say anything. Dad took the English exercise books out and said, "Lucky you, it's clear today."

He placed the books on the ground outside the room and covered them with some waste newspaper.

The next day the books were all dry. Dad reviewed them word by word, sentence by sentence. I was expecting Dad to give me a small compliment. But he did not. Not a single word. He finished correcting my exercise and said, "The best gift you can give to me is your exercises. What is fermented bean curd for?"

The only thing that crossed my mind at the time was that Dad was cold. I attempted to upset him. I said, "Easier said than done. Studying English is not allowed. No English materials are available in any stores. What do you want to me to do?"

Dad interrupted me, "The *Complete Works of Mao* is available in English."

I felt outraged. "I don't have spare money for such stupid books."

"Nothing is stupid as long as it can help you learn something. The English version of Mao's collections is idiomatic."

Dad crawled under the bed and pulled out a wooden trunk. He took a book out and handed it to me. "Here is my English version of Mao's works. I bought it before I left Beijing. It's yours now. Studying English is forbidden. Studying Mao's teachings is not. There is a Chinese set of Mao's works at home. You can study English by reading both versions."

What else could I say? When I returned to work, I read the Chinese version when the leaders of the factory were present. Otherwise I read the English version.

Gradually the leaders began to think of me as a good youth, trying to reform myself and willing to break off my relationship with my father. I impressed them with my study of Mao's teachings. They even considered transferring me to a better job.

I thought my life had come to a turning point, that society might look at me now as an individual human being without checking my family background first. But I rejoiced too soon.

One day I had just gotten home from work when Sun's father came over. I knew immediately that something bad was about to happen. Sun's father had come to our home before the Cultural Revolution had ruined our lives but never since my dad and mom had been sent away. He was part of the Rebel organization that had persecuted Dad and his intellectual colleagues.

He started the conversation with a question: "Did you recently run into Sun at the gate of our apartment building?"

"Yes I did," I said. "Why?"

"What did you say to him?"

"Nothing special."

"Did you pat him on the head?"

"I don't remember. Maybe."

"I know you did," he said, irritated, adding, "It's been on his mind ever since. He's been whispering about it for a month. You have to go to see him. He's sick again. Do not tell Sun I asked you to come."

I knew he was blaming me for Sun's sickness. I knew I had to go see his son. The father had become a powerful person and could cause my parents problems if I didn't cooperate. I agreed to come see Sun. He told me to come to his sister's house. Sun would be there the next day.

I arrived at Sun's aunt's house late the next afternoon. When he saw me walk in, Sun jumped up from the bamboo chair where he had been sitting.

"Why are you here?" Sun asked.

"Oh, I just stopped by," I answered. "One of my old teachers lives in this compound. I just came from his house."

I stayed to chat for about fifteen minutes. When I was ready to leave, Sun insisted on following me to the bus stop. His father said that he would join us.

On the way to the bus stop, Sun suddenly stopped walking. He said he wanted to compare heights with me to see who was taller. He pushed me behind him and turned to stand back to back. His father patted our heads a bit and said to him, "You are taller, my son."

"Sure, you are taller than I am. And stronger than I am also," I said. As matter of a fact, I had grown much taller than Sun.

This seemed to please Sun. My bus pulled up and opened its door. As I climbed aboard, Sun pushed his way onto the bus behind me. Putting his hand on the top of my head, he said, "You need to get your hair cut."

Gazing at the two receding figures out the bus window, I realized why Sun's father asked me to visit his son. He wanted me to be touched on the head by his son in public. I was caught by a feeling of sadness and hopelessness. Just because my father had political problems meant that my life could be controlled by someone else, someone like Sun and his father. Their "political reliability" was no justification for their abusive power. I told myself everything would be fine with me, and I could protect Dad's future if I would cooperate with Sun's parents to recover his health. Then Sun would appreciate my cooperation, and his parents would treat my parents a little more nicely.

What happened to me a week later proved I was wrong. I was off that day when Sun's mother came to my house. She said her son wanted to talk to me and I must go. The tone of her voice was like a military order. I went.

When I arrived, Sun suggested, "Lingmu, let's go for a walk. Just in the courtyard of the newspaper."

"Your mother said you want to talk to me." I was puzzled.

"We can talk while walking." Sun dragged me out his house.

As we were walking toward the newspaper compound, he suddenly asked, "Are we good friends?"

"I think so," I said, not quite understanding what he meant.

"Then you have to give me a horsey-back ride," he said, wearing a strange smile.

"That's impossible!" I felt terribly insulted. "I won't do that no matter what you do."

"You should know that because of you I am ill," he threatened me, "and do not forget that your father is a traitor. If you will not let me ride you like a horse, I am going to tell my father."

I was afraid of his father's power, but what Sun wanted of me would cost me my dignity as a human being.

Sun said the canteen would open soon. It was dinnertime and a lot of people would go to the canteen. He claimed that he would help me save face by pretending to have a fight with me. I would fall down on the ground, and he would jump on my back.

I agreed.

Soon people began to rush in and out of the canteen. Sun and I started pushing each other back and forth. Our "battle" drew five or six kids our age. Sun looked around. He suddenly tripped me, and I fell to the ground. Being really tripped was not part of our plan. I was so insulted I tried to get back up, but Sun was on my back before I could do so.

Riding on my back, he grabbed my shirt in one hand and my hair in the another. He screamed, "Run quickly, you *gouzaizi*."[2]

"I beg you; do not make me crawl on the ground like a dog anymore," I said to Sun. "Other people have seen us. They all know you are by far better than I am at everything."

Sun refused to get off, however, until one of the crowd stepped in. He thought Sun and I were having a real fight.

"Stop it now!" He tried to separate us by dragging Sun off my back. "You, get off him. You have beaten him. You won the fight, and I am your witness."

I have never been so insulted in my whole life. Nevertheless, I had to take it quietly for my parents' sake. I comforted myself with the idea that it was really over this time. I had taken the worst Sun could demand—touching my head in public as though I were a little child, riding me like a horse. Even if there was something I should feel guilt for, Sun should feel that the score was even now.

Life was so unpredictable. A week after our fight Sun committed suicide by drinking a powerful insecticide. He left a note for his parents

---

2. *Gouzaizi* (figuratively, "son of a bitch") was a form of address created by the Rebels for the children whose parents had been denounced by the Party.

that said, "Lingmu's dad is a traitor. And he is a *gouzaizi*. Why should he be better than I am?"

Even though all this happened years ago, once in a while Sun's parents still mention his death, hinting that I am somehow responsible. I do not feel guilty. The only thing that worries me sometimes is the idea that something like the Cultural Revolution might return. If that happened, would I be labeled a murderer who got away? What a terrible thing that would be for my child.

NO ADOLESCENCE

In June 1992, I was traveling through Tokyo and stopped to visit an old friend, Mingzi. When I told her I was writing a book about the Cultural Revolution, she suggested I interview a friend of hers in Beijing, Zhanhua. Mingzi warned me not to interview Zhanhua at home. "You need to watch out for her mother," she said. "She doesn't like pretty women like you. You should get Zhanhua to tell you why."

Mingzi showed me an old picture of Zhanhua's mother. She was a beautiful woman. From this photo, I developed a picture of Zhanhua in my mind—a beautiful young lady, fastidious about her clothing and appearance. When she first appeared at the door of my hotel room in Beijing, she was not what I imagined.

I had never seen a Chinese woman with such an exotic, Eurasian air about her. Zhanhua has deep, hazel eyes; a large nose; and fair skin.[1] Her hair is peculiar among the black-haired crowds in Beijing: a color between blonde and red.

In opposition to her looks, however, she was dressed head to toe in old, almost shabby clothing. She was wearing a wrinkled, off-white dress and dingy, high-heeled white sandals. Her shoulder-length hair was tied back in a ponytail. She obviously cared nothing for her looks or for the kind of first impression she made on people.

I do not remember having an adolescence—I went from being a little girl straight to being a full-grown woman. Every time I see teenage girls

---

1. Large noses are considered an attractive Western trait by the Chinese.

in pretty clothes giggling in front of a department store underwear counter, I wonder why I had to miss that wonderful period of my life. Those young ladies look so mature, confident, and proud of their bodies when they examine the lacy panties and push-up, underwire brassieres. They are not even bashful when the salesperson behind the counter is male.

When I go home, I see my mother sitting on the sofa, a rag doll just dropped. Nothing about her could make you believe she was elegant and beautiful when she was young.

If I walk into the living room, my mother's look makes me automatically drop my shoulders and feel ashamed of myself. I never hold my head high or throw out my chest like those teenage girls. My mother's look has controlled me since I was a teenager. Her beauty and the problems it caused her shadowed my childhood and ruined my adolescence. She was a victim of the Cultural Revolution, and her persecution haunts my life to this day.

I was eleven when my father was accused of being a traitor and pulled down from his position in the municipal court system. It was 1967. Following my father's dismissal, my mother was also expelled from her position. She was also accused of being *huacheng meinu de she* [a snake in the disguise of a beautiful woman]. Her head was shaved in the *ying yang tou* style that leaves one half of the head shaved and the other half closely cropped. It made a beautiful woman ugly.

The Rebels took my mother to a public mass meeting for criticism and denunciation. When she was finally allowed to come home, she was still wearing a wooden board hung around her neck. The board showed a snake in a flashy dress and high-heeled red shoes. The snake had big breasts. The caption read, " I confess. I am a snake in the disguise of a beautiful woman."

I had just finished taking a bath as my mother came into the house. I was combing my hair in front of her dresser mirror. I liked to look into that mirror and imagine I was Red Riding Hood. My hair was different from most Chinese. For some unknown reason, I had light hair. Nobody ever figured out where I got my hair color, and no one had ever criticized me for its color or shine. Instead, everyone complimented me. They gave me the nickname "Yang Wawa" (Western Doll).

This time I did not see that cute little girl. Instead, I saw my mother standing in the bedroom door staring at me. I was about to greet her when she pulled one of the drawers out of her dresser and spilled it across the bed. Grabbing a pair of scissors, she pulled me down on the bed and began to cut off my hair. I tried to resist her, but my small body failed me. As she cut my hair, she repeated, "I let you be beautiful. I let you be beautiful." She did not stopping cutting until my hair was cut to my ears.

Looking into the mirror, I started to cry. That young lady with the hair that hung to her waist was gone, and I looked like an ugly boy.

I think people like to look beautiful. It's something in their nature. But that sense was killed in me by my mother. And as soon as she took those scissors to my head, my love for my beautiful mother was also gone, gone with my hair.

Mother walked out the room, leaving the words in the air, "You will thank your mother for cutting your hair someday. Someday soon." I looked at the back of mother's *yin yang tou* and then glanced at the snake painted on the wooden board she dropped in the corner, trying to figure out the connection between my haircut and my mother's haircut, between my mother and the snake. I could not make sense of anything, but I learned by instinct that beauty was a bad thing and that beautiful women were automatically criminals.

Soon after my haircut, the Party sent my parents to a poor area in the middle of the Shaanxi loess plateau. The Party claimed it was for their own good.

In the winter of 1969, a year and a half after my parents were sent away, the six of us children were sent to the same village. The trip took two days via train and bus, but I was happy. I knew that from the time I was reunited with my parents, I would be protected from all those children who scorned me, called me names, and spit in my face. I would no longer be an orphan.

I remember the way my mother's eyes looked when she beheld her six children, the youngest now ten years old, standing in front of the cave where she existed with my father. She just stared at us, not even responding when I called out to her.

Once I saw her expressionless face, I realized that neither of my parents would give us any protection. My parents' situation was like that of a "clay idol fording a river"—they were hardly able to help themselves.

My older sister and brother seemed to understand our parents' situation. They put our belongs on the *kang* where mother said we would sleep.[2] I could not believe that all of us would fit on that *kang*.

At home we all had our own beds. My bed had a wooden frame and a soft mattress. I also used to have a maid who would tease me, saying, I was a little princess as she made the bed for me. After a look at that *kang*, I suddenly missed my bedroom and my bed at home, forgetting all the scary nights alone.

There was no electricity, no running water, and no toilet inside the cave. The *kang* was supposed to be warmed up before bedtime, but because of the shortage of fuel in the countryside, it never got warm enough. We slept wearing every piece of clothing we possessed.

The cold hardness of the *kang* together with the embarrassment of sleeping in the same bed with my brothers kept me from falling asleep the entire first night. All night I kept telling myself that I was going back to Beijing. I imagined that I could walk back as long as I stuck to the railroad tracks.

As soon as the sun was up, I slipped out of the cave. Outside was a boundless stretch of yellow earth. The emptiness made me lose my sense of direction. There was no dividing line between the sky and the earth, no way to tell where the yellow earth ended and the yellow sky began. And there was no railway track. The surroundings frightened me. I knew I would never get back to Beijing and my whole life would be spent on the endless yellow earth.

---

2. A *kang* is a sleeping platform made of brick, which is heated from the underside.

Soon my mother came out of the cave and told me it was my job to fetch water from the "local" well—over a mile a way. I was terrified I would get lost, but she had no patience. "Go directly south and you will find the well," she said. She showed me a flatbed cart with an old petroleum barrel lashed to it with wire. "Take this," she said. It wasn't so difficult to pull on the way to the well. But the way back was the uphill road to hell. The road was narrow and I learned the meaning of the phrase *yangchang xiaotao* [meandering footpath]. I had only heard this phrase in movies and books. Now I was actually struggling up such a narrow, winding trail.

It would not have been so bad if the path was just rough. However, I also had to deal with the wind. It made a piercing cry like a hungry wolf. The air was so dry that I could hear my skin cracking. I had no gloves, and my hands were soon frozen to the handles of the flatbed. I had no idea how to free my hands, but I knew I had to set them free so that I could put them in my pockets and get warm before my fingers fell off. I pulled as hard as I could and my hands came free, but some skin peeled off my palms and stuck to the handles. My palms were bleeding. I tried to take off my shirt to wrap my hands, but then I was afraid I would die in the cold weather.

There were no plants to pick leaves from. The only thing still on the earth was dried wild grass, the same yellow color as the dirt. The only thing I could do was to continue to pull the flatbed home. I closed my eyes and counted—one, two, three. I grabbed the handles, bent into the wind, and headed home.

My mother was standing by the door of the cave gazing at the barren countryside as I came up the path. There was no hint of sympathy for my bloody hands. "You do not know all there is to know about life," she said. I was not certain if she was talking to me or to herself.

"This is the truth of life," she said, pointing at my hands. "Rough skin and ugly, shabby clothing are protection for women." Soon I realized that what my mother said was not just her comments on life; they were her requirements for all her children, especially my sisters and myself.

We never got the chance to take a bath. Soon I found myself struggling with lice. So did my sisters. It got so bad that I was often unable to sleep at night. I told my mother that we needed to take a bath. "Those lice are really nothing," she replied. "You shouldn't be so squeamish." She acted like the lice were nothing more than dandruff on my shoulders. "Think about the local peasants. They all have lice," she said.

For the first month we were in the countryside I wished for a bath every night when I went to bed. However, I soon had more than lice and baths to worry about. One morning when I woke up I noticed that there was blood on my underwear. I did not understand what it was, and I did not know what I should do about it. I did not dare tell my mother. I could not turn to my older sister either because I felt shy and ashamed. Without knowing what to do, I cut the crotch out of my underwear and washed the rest. After my underwear dried, I cut a piece of cloth from some other clothes I had and mended them. I did this every day for a week. My mother became very cross and complained, "How could you possibly wear out a pair of underwear every day?" I wish my mother would have been sensitive enough to ask me what was happening to me.

That was it. My passage to adolescence.

The next time when I found the blood, I was more experienced, although I still felt something mysterious and scary was going on. I discovered the sanitary towel my mother used. I cut a hole in my cotton sleeping pad, dug some cotton out, and put it in a towel. For five years I consumed the cotton in my sleeping pad. Oh, poor mattress. It was full of holes by the time we moved back to Beijing.

My adolescent experiences made me not only feel strange but also act strangely. I had a coin with a square hole at the middle, strung on a red thread. I swung the coin for the entire week of my monthly period whenever I went for walks because I did not want anyone, including my family members, to get close to me. Each month I wished my mother would noticed my weird behavior and talk to me, but she never did.

However, my mother did notice another change in my body. My breasts were developing. Instinct told me this was not a good thing. I remembered the snake placard my mother had around her neck. The snake had big breasts. I began walking with my shoulders hunched forward to change my profile. One morning after I came home from fetching the water, I took off my sweater, leaving just my shirt on. All of a sudden I felt my mother looking at me from the other end of the cave. Her look was so powerful and penetrating that I put my sweater back on. "What did I teach you?" mother said. "Don't you ever stand or walk like that again."

"Like what?" I was confused.

"With your chin up and your chest sticking out."

"I did not have my chest out," I said, but she refused to listen. She continued to watch me, always checking to see if I held my chest out. Her look clearly said that being a woman was bad and being a pretty woman was worse. Her look was effective. I believed my mother's look was for my sake, so I did not disappoint her. During the night, I beat my breasts. I thought if I beat them hard enough, they would stop growing. During the day, I wrapped my breasts tightly with a piece of cloth cut from my sheets.

I think my efforts resulted in the flat chest I have now. But that never stopped my mother's looks. I could tell that she felt that she had committed a crime in giving birth to me because I constantly reminded her of her past as a beautiful woman. This realization led me to see that when adults suffer something they cannot bear, they transfer their feelings and fears to their children.

Even today my mother continues to sit in that living room and give me her looks. I don't blame her. Her beauty ruined her life, and it ruined my girlhood.

POSTSCRIPT

ALL OF MY FRIENDS from my childhood have stories about the Cultural Revolution and what it did to their lives. Unlike others of our generation, those with the working-class and peasant backgrounds that allowed them to join the Red Guards, as children of parents in the Black categories we were disempowered by the Cultural Revolution, stripped of our dignity and our futures. Some of us have managed to salvage something of a present from the tatters of our lives that we were left with at the end of the 1970s, but none of us is whole. Many of us lost one or both of our parents to the excesses of the Red Guards or to the harsh conditions of the reform through labor camps. All of us lost precious years when we could and should have been studying for our life's work. Now in our thirties and forties, we struggle to catch up, to make up for that lost time.

When I set out to write this book, I constantly encountered the same question from people in China (and from Chinese in America): "Why do you want to write about *that* part of history? No one wants to hear those old stories."

When my friends asked this question, their voices were filled with complex feelings: impatience, anger, concern. Most of all, however, their voices held accusations. They seemed to be saying, "I am all right now. Don't drag me back to the horrible old days." I am one of them. I understand their feelings. I am willing to suffer their criticism, willing to open up the closed wounds, exposing the still painful flesh beneath the scar.

166

However, nothing I experienced during the Cultural Revolution, or after in my five years as a reporter, prepared me for the pain my Chinese friends felt when recalling those years for me. At first they were all reluctant to open the sealed past. It was only when I told them I would write their stories so that they would be heard by the outside world that many decided to open their hearts to me. The telling made it seem as though the events had just taken place rather than happening some twenty years before. The women cried uncontrollably; the men fought back their tears.

I felt guilty for making them experience their nightmares again. I wanted to give up a couple of times—not just for their sake, but also for my own because I was reexperiencing the nightmares as well. However, something deep in my heart kept encouraging me to continue moving down this sad emotional road.

When I look at myself in the mirror, or into the eyes of my brothers and sisters, I see the confused and cynical, responsible, older, and yet still-loyal faces of the once-much-younger us. I do not want the same innocent, flowering faces of my children and their children to be frightened and distorted by the events of youth. My brothers and sisters agree with me, so they have told me their stories. The stories are, in part, a legacy to their children, letting them know and remember what we were and where we came from.

My work here has been to translate those stories from the voices of my friends to the page and from Chinese to English. All translation runs the risk of damaging the original text. I realize this, and I have tried here to translate those voices without doing too much damage to them. What I hope I have done is salvage something from those years, recovering the stories so that the pain and suffering do not go totally to waste. My friends and I suffered in the dark for many years. It is time to bring that pain into the light.

To some, these stories may be exotic, but to the intellectuals and their children who lived through the Cultural Revolution, the stories will be quite familiar. The Cultural Revolution swept every corner of the country and shook every family. Everyone has her or his own history, but the history of what happened to individuals and families doesn't belong to us as individuals anymore.

I understand that life goes on, that most members of my generation now have families. They have to deal with the hard reality of raising their children and making a living in an increasingly complex and competitive world. No one can afford to live in the past. However, it does not matter how wonderful or difficult life is today or might be tomorrow. Our present is always linked with our past. We can forget all the opportunities we missed to be honored, wealthy, or glamorous, but we should not forget the calamities we suffered as individuals and as a society.

When everyone is involved in the same historical event in the way we all were during the Cultural Revolution, each small, individual story reflects our national history. By telling our individual stories, we make sense of our collective experience.

Memory is a wreath made of the different incidents in a life. It does not matter whether the incidents are horrible or sweet; we make the wreath by picking out the incidents that touch our hearts the most. The Cultural Revolution was extremely cruel, but my brothers and sisters and I cannot leave it out of our wreath. Our wreath might not be as beautiful or perfect as we would like it to be, but it is our life.

About the Book and Author

These evocative stories bring to life the tragic personal impact of the Cultural Revolution on the families of China's intellectuals. Now adults, survivors recall their childhood during the tumultuous years between 1965 and 1976, when Mao's death finally drew a curtain on a bitterly failed social and political experiment.

A series of first-person narratives eloquently describes the life-long influence of this seminal period on China's children. Those who were teenagers in the late 1960s joined the Red Guards and the revolutionary rebel groups, following Mao's directives to make revolution, often to their own undoing. Those who were too young to participate directly were even more vulnerable. Although they had little understanding of the political firestorm that engulfed their parents, they were old enough to understand and feel the terror it brought. Vividly capturing the emotional intensity of the time, these stories explore what it was like to be caught up in revolutionary fervor, to be sent to the countryside, to be separated—either ideologically or physically—from one's parents, often forever.

By undermining families and family structure, the Cultural Revolution created a generation of Chinese who view politics, the Communist Party, and life itself with deep cynicism. Presenting a spectrum of individual stories of people who saw the Cultural Revolution through the eyes of a child, *The Red Mirror* offers rare insights for understanding the crippling legacy of the Cultural Revolution.

CHIHUA WEN is a former editor and reporter for the Xinhua News Agency in Beijing. She earned an M.A. in Sociology from the University of California at

San Diego and an M.A. in Asian Studies from San Diego State University. She is currently a freelance writer whose work is regularly published in both magazines and newspapers in China. Her work covers a wide variety of social issues in China. She also writes about cultural issues in the United States.

Printed in the United States
38976LVS00002B/32